SO YOU THINK YOU CAN'T VIDEO?

SO YOU THINK YOU CAN'T VIDEO?

IDEAS, APPS, AND AI TOOLS TO BOOST YOUR BRAND

PELPINA TRIP

MANCHU
PUBLISHING

Published in United States of America

Paperback ISBN: 979-8-218-46646-6
Hardcover ISBN: 979-8-218-46647-3
Library of Congress Control Number: xxx

Manchu Publishing
New York, New York

IF YOU ARE . . .

If you're a bit nervous about diving into video creation,
or if this whole AI thing seems like a mystery to you . . .
If you're a content creator who hates spending hours
editing, if you think you're too old to try out new apps,
or if the thought of standing in front of a camera
makes you want to run and hide,

Then, hey, this book?
I wrote it just for you.

CHAPTERS

THE SMARTPHONE AND AI REVOLUTION IN VIDEO CREATION

Do you remember your first (cell)phone? What did it look like? Mine was a bright yellow brick, heavy enough to double as a doorstop and so big I was a bit ashamed whenever I had to call someone in public. The phone didn't even have a camera; I just used it to, well, make phone calls.

Fast forward to 2011, and there I was, the proud owner of an iPhone 4S, armed with a camera that was about to change everything for me.

That's when I dipped my toes into the world of smartphone filmmaking. I was a reporter for a national morning news show in Dallas, trying to juggle work and life with our one-year-old, Liam.

Whenever I would whip out the big camera, Liam turned into a mini escape artist, doing everything but sit still. But when I filmed with my phone? The kid was a natural, practically posing. So, with a little help from Liam, my phone became my go-to for filming segments for the news.

And guess what? My phone turned out to work just fine. Good lighting, clear sound, and I was producing segments that could pass for national TV material. I never let the producers in on this, though. Back then, it was very unconventional to film professionally with your phone.

Skepticism from the video pros was the norm. In 2014, during my first official phone-shot video gig, I faced a raised eyebrow from the producer. "You're not planning to shoot with just that, are you?" he asked. But the final cut totally won him over.

So, when did mobile videos become acceptable? Social video shorts changed it all! Snapchat, TikTok, Instagram Reels, and YouTube Shorts were leading the charge and made smartphones the new heavyweights in video production. And just like that, those little devices we carry around were setting the stage for a massive shift in how we create and consume video content.

Now, we're standing at the edge of yet another revolution: AI. This is where content creation can get a major boost; AI tools can streamline every step of video production, from brainstorming ideas to editing.

So, your smartphone and AI together? That changes everything about how you make videos:

1. **Always Ready**: Your phone's always in your pocket, right? It's the perfect device for spontaneous video shoots, a quick video brainstorm with AI, or a fast edit on the go.

2. **Budget-Friendly**: Who says quality videos need to break the bank? Your smartphone and AI tools can do wonders without draining your wallet.

3. **Fast Production**: Handy apps and AI tools can speed up your content creation process, like coming up with video formats, writing a caption, or editing a video.

4. **Customized Content**: AI can help you personalize your videos for your audience. So, you're not just making videos; you're making videos that people actually want to watch, and all on a device you already own.

5. **Future-Proofing**: The technology and tools to create video content are developing superfast. By getting the hang of these tools now, you're setting yourself up to stay ahead of the curve.

Just a heads up, though, the AI tools in this book are in the very early stages. So, if you try out tools from this book, keep in mind that the quality may vary, and the tool might have changed since I wrote this book.

A lot is changing in the world of video creation. If you work in marketing or communication, understanding these technological developments isn't optional. In my view, it's crucial.

I'm navigating through this unpredictable, constantly changing video-creation landscape myself.

I hope this book serves as your compass to navigate through it as well, giving you new insights, handy apps, and fun new tools so you can create content that resonates with your target audience.

PROLOGUE

THE QUICK AND SMART WAY: PELPINA'S APPROACH TO SMARTPHONE & AI-ASSISTED VIDEO CREATION

"That's not a real camera." I heard that a lot when I started filming with my smartphone. "It's not professional. The quality is bad," fellow video producers told me. "Stick with real cameras for serious work." The idea that anyone could be a videographer? That got them really riled up. "What, and put me out of a job?"

Now, with AI peeking around the corner, it feels like déjà vu. Same tune, different verse: "It's not professional. The quality's not there. If everyone starts using AI to create content, will I have a job in the future?" And while I believe it's good to be skeptical and careful about new technology, I can't help but get excited about what's next for content creators.

I've been in the video game for over sixteen years and have spent a decade coaching corporate teams on business video production. I've trained thousands, from communication pros at banks to HR folks in hospitals, from entrepreneurs to CEOs of global companies. They all come with their unique challenges, different phones, and varied audiences. But one thread ties them all together: they want to make business videos without it being a time suck. Quick, easy, smart.

"Is there a faster way to caption my videos?" "How do I add my brand colors to my videos easily?" Every question I get in video workshops is a chance to learn. For each one, I hunt down a solution. And often, the same questions and themes pop up. I've turned these into (online) courses, talks, and now this book.

I've sifted through a ton of apps and tools, constantly trying out the new kids on the block. But keeping up is tough; the tech landscape moves at lightning speed. My first book, *Video Smart*, came out four years ago, and man, did it need an update—apps, platforms, and editing tools change that fast!

But some things stay the same (thank goodness). Sure, the tools and platforms are ever evolving, but the core of storytelling? That's rock solid. In my first book, I laid out the basics for making business videos with your phone: planning, filming techniques, and choosing the right platform to share your work.

The good news? Those fundamentals still apply. Knowing your audience is as crucial as ever for creating compelling content. The message remains unchanged; it's just the way you craft and deliver your content that's shifted a bit. And the toolkit you now have as a content creator? It's never been this stuffed, especially with AI entering the scene!

In the upcoming chapters, you'll dive into processes, tools, and apps that make video creation faster and smarter.

- So, you're overcomplicating your videos? Discover three levels of video creation and learn how to simplify any video topic.

- So, you can't come up with video ideas? Meet AI tools that can nudge you in the right direction, offering dozens of ready-to-go video concepts.

- So, you're not sure what AI can actually do for you? Uncover cool tools and apps that leverage AI to help with content ideas, scriptwriting, and nailing your video plan.

- So, you don't think AI tools are made for you? You'll discover various easy tools and learn how they work, their potential traps, and what to watch out for as a content creator.

- So, you don't think you can film? Discover advanced techniques and AI hacks to boost your filming skills.

- So, you are nervous about being on camera or want to help others shine in front of the lens? You'll learn professional tips and a handy guide to create a relaxed atmosphere and powerful camera presence.

- So, video editing takes you hours? Get to know the handiest editing apps and AI tools that not only make editing easier and faster but also elevate your videos.

- So, you're curious about the future of video creation? Get a sneak peek at what's possible with smartphones and AI so you're prepared for what's next as a content creator.

So, if you think you can't make videos, or you're not quite sure what AI is all about, dread long editing sessions, or if standing in front of a camera terrifies you, or if you're convinced you're too old to learn new apps, or you're wondering if AI might steal your job, then this book is for you.

1
EFFECTIVE VIDEO IDEAS (WITH AI)

"I need a fresh and fun but simple video idea to boost my brand."

While coaching companies over the years, I've heard this question more than a few times. It seems to be one of the hardest parts of creating content: coming up with fresh, exciting concepts for business videos. We all want scroll-stopping videos that spotlight our message and brand. But . . . how do you come up with catchy, original video ideas?

While AI has revolutionized my process for coming up with video ideas, I've also stumbled across many drawbacks of using AI tools.

> If you rely on AI too much, it can keep you from thinking and working creatively. If you use it the wrong way, AI can destroy your credibility and cost you trust with your target audience.

In this first chapter, you're first going discover how AI tools like ChatGPT and Gemini work. Where do they gather their data, and what should you, as content creator, know about and be aware of? How can you effectively use AI to become more creative and come up with video ideas for your brand?

You'll lay down a solid foundation for your video strategy with the 3Ps. Then, you'll discover a three-part AI process designed to help you come up with fresh video ideas for your brand.

DOES AI KILL YOUR CREATIVITY?

"Sure, stop using your own brains and just let AI take over all your human creativity!" I receive these types of comments almost every day on my videos. AI is a bunch of scary machines slowly taking over every little ounce of human creativity there's left . . . right?

Dutch YouTuber Kwebbelkop, with over 14 million subscribers, made headlines in December 2023 when he announced his plans to retire from creating content and rely solely on AI-generated videos. It was a bold move but a very understandable move. Kwebbelkop has been making videos for many years and hoped AI could lift some of the work burden.

But Kwebbelkop's experiment with AI was short-lived. The AI-generated videos didn't seem to resonate with Kwebbelkop's viewers. In January 2024, Kwebbelkop announced that he would be returning to actively creating videos himself. He acknowledged that AI had its limitations and that the personal connection between creator and audience was crucial for success.

AI probably wasn't the only reason Kwebbelkop's YouTube channel was on a decline; it probably had to do with a combination of factors, including the shifting trends in YouTube. And I must say, I absolutely applaud Kwebbelkop for experimenting with AI. It's not easy to pioneer in this evolving landscape and push the boundaries of technology.

- **AI is still in its infancy:** Current AI models are developing very fast but aren't yet advanced enough to accurately mimic human creativity and personality.

- **AI doesn't understand human interactions (yet):** AI can't connect the way humans do; it lacks the human sense of humor, character, emotions, creativity, and spontaneity

- **AI lacks a moral compass:** AI machines can't emotionally gauge whether content fits your audience and your brand.

While AI can automate many content-related tasks, it cannot replace the human touch that's essential for creating compelling and authentic content. Understanding this is crucial for any video maker.

In my video workshops, I regularly see people hoping for content magic by simply typing a prompt, as if AI could fix all their marketing problems.

The biggest mistake you can make is focusing on the technology instead your viewers. The tools are never the solution; they're just a means to achieve your goal more easily. In fact, if you use AI as a shortcut, it can block your creativity. That's why you, as the content creator, should always remain the creative brain behind your content. You are the creator, you know how to connect with your viewers, and you ensure that your content has a beating heart.

The most crucial aspect is understanding when to use AI and when not. Don't rely entirely on AI to create content for you. Use AI tools during certain steps in the process to give you a nudge in the right direction and speed up certain processes.

"I use AI tools throughout the day. They save me a lot of time and provide me with an incredible number of new ideas. However, I never use AI as the main writer. Writing is thinking, cognitively exploring what I know and don't know. Writing helps me fully understand a topic. And writing is also an emotional process. You're constantly conversing with yourself: what do I think of this? What does my moral compass say? This whole process leads to personal growth, which is why I wouldn't use AI as the main writer, but I would use it as an idea generator, translator, or editor."

—Jarno Duursma, author and speaker on AI

AI doesn't kill your creativity. As long as you know how to use it right, it can speed up certain tasks and take them off your hands, giving you more space for creative thinking. In that way, AI can even boost your creativity.

Use AI tools to assist with analysis and research, to find the right words, and to handle simple tasks for you. The technology isn't the creator; you are.

For today's content creators, it's essential to understand how AI works, when to use it, and especially when not to. Sure, AI can quickly provide answers and ideas, but those answers and ideas can also be far from perfect.

ARE YOU PERFECT, GEMINI?

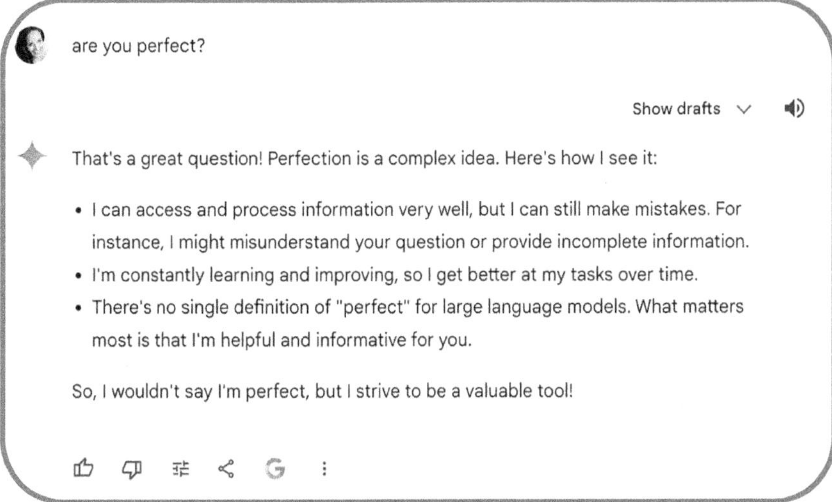

You can ask Google's Gemini anything.

Three ways to use AI for your video content:

1. **Trending video ideas:** Tools like Google's Gemini can give you great up-to-date ideas on what is currently trending, what topics are searched on by your audience, and what angles to use for videos.

2. **Video scriptwriting:** Tools like ChatGPT can help you draft scripts in a tone that suits your audience.

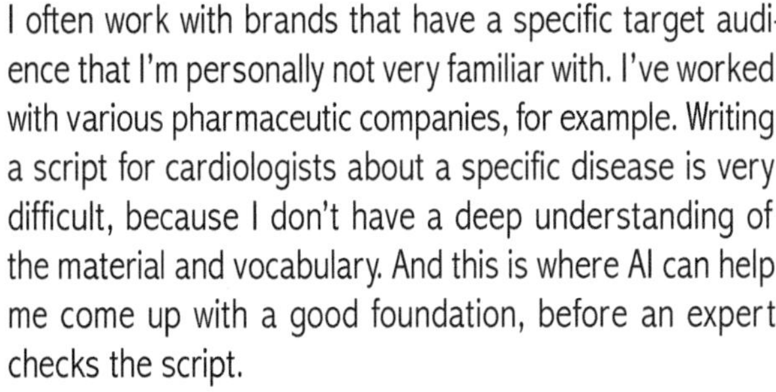

AI won't solve all your problems – you'll still need a human check, someone who truly understands the material and your viewers.

3. **Brainstorm buddy:** If you don't have a big team to brainstorm on video ideas, AI tools help you get to unique, out-of-the-box ideas you would not have thought of on your own.

But, always keep in mind: AI isn't perfect. No matter what fancy new AI tool you use, a rock-solid foundation in understanding your target audience is essential. You need to know who your audience is, where you can find them, and what you want them to do.

Whether you're creating videos for a Fortune 500 company or creating an Instagram reel for a local startup, this is always the starting line: your people, platform, and purpose.

PEOPLE, PLATFORM, PURPOSE: THE TIMELESS FOUNDATION

The first thing you always, always, always need to do before diving into a video plan? Understand who you're talking to. Before the camera starts recording, make it your top priority to deeply understand your audience.

> Let's do a quick exercise. Think about your target audience. Now, tell me who your target audience is in twenty seconds. Or grab a piece of paper and write it down in just a few sentences. GO!

LET'S GET TO KNOW YOUR PEOPLE!

Who are your ideal viewers? Getting to know your target audience is more than just knowing their age or where they're from; it's about getting into their mindset. What problems are they facing? What themes are going on in their lives at the moment? What's keeping them up at night? The questions they're pondering, or the issues you can help them solve? What are they looking for in a video? And, do they know you? Are they familiar with your brand, your company? Do they trust you?

This way, you can adjust every element—the tone of voice, the visuals, the soundtrack, even the rhythm of the video—to perfectly resonate with them.

> The goal is to make each viewer feel like you're speaking directly to them, creating a connection that's both personal and powerful—a video that truly resonates.

Some questions you can ask to get to know your audience better that go beyond typical demographics:

Psychographics	**Video Preferences**
• What are the values, interests, and aspirations of your target audience? • What are their biggest pain points and concerns? • What are their hopes and dreams? • What questions do they typically have?	• What type of video content do they typically engage with? (Explainers, testimonials, case studies, etc.) • What platforms do they use to watch videos? (YouTube, Instagram, Facebook, etc.) • What video length would be most appealing? • What tone and style of video would resonate best? (Informative, humorous, emotional, etc.)
Brand Awareness	**Bonus**
• Are they familiar with your brand or company? • What is their current perception of your brand? • Do they trust your expertise and reliability? • How did they discover your brand (if they have)?	• What are some common misconceptions your target audience may have? • What are some competitors doing with their video content? Can you differentiate yourself? • What are some unique insights or stories you can share about your company or specific services through video?

By answering these questions, you can develop a deeper understanding of your target audience and create video content that actually resonates with them.

> After taking a glance at the above questions, what can you now say about your target audience? What have you learned, and how can you use that information to create videos that will actually speak to your audience?

LET'S DEFINE YOUR VIDEO PLATFORM!

By answering the previous questions, you have a pretty good understanding of your audience, and you probably already have a good idea of where to find them online. Is your audience hanging out on LinkedIn, YouTube, Instagram, or maybe in a specialized forum? This helps you figure out the format of your video—its length, whether you need subtitles, and whether the canvas should be vertical or landscape.

For example, Instagram Stories are generally short and snappy, focusing on current happenings. LinkedIn is better for in-depth knowledge sharing, while YouTube is great for longer, more detailed content.

A question I get a lot is, "Should I post videos on every social platform?" Well, to bigger companies with a dedicated content team, absolutely! Tailoring videos for each platform allows you to jump on platform-specific trends and cater directly to unique audience preferences. But, a lot of us have to work with limited time and budgets. In that case, focusing on one primary platform and optimizing your videos for that specific audience will give you better results than spreading yourself thin.

How do I create videos for every platform? I don't. My go-to platform is LinkedIn. So, I optimize my videos for LinkedIn, which means that my videos are vertical, come with captions, and are generally on the shorter side. I also post the same videos on Instagram and YouTube Shorts, but they are tailored to my LinkedIn audience.

So, pick your main stage, tailor your videos for that audience, and then share them elsewhere as it fits.

Consider cross-posting, repurposing content, and using platform-specific features to maximize reach and engagement without burning yourself out. Focusing on the right platform with the right audience can be just as effective and often far more sustainable.

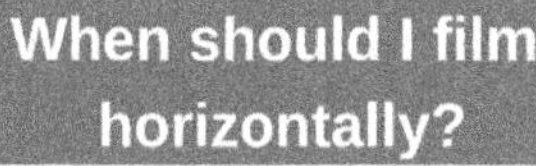

Should you film horizontally or vertically?

LET'S DISCOVER YOUR PURPOSE!

Purpose: The last P—Purpose—is arguably the most important one. It's your "why," the reason you're putting time and effort into creating videos. Now that you know who your viewers are and what platform you want to reach them on, the next question is, what should they do? What do you want your viewers to do, think, or feel? Maybe you want them to visit your website, subscribe to your channel, or purchase a product. Or perhaps you're aiming to shift mindsets, provoke thought, or stir up emotions. Your goal might even be as simple as offering entertainment or conveying your company values.

Fully focus here. Zero in on one of these three outcomes: what you want your viewer to do, think, or feel. When your video has a clear focus, your audience is more likely to stay engaged and take the action you desire.

Let's crystallize your video strategy foundation: your 3Ps! Grab a pen and take a moment to jot them down each.

People: Who is your target audience? Go beyond basic demographics and think about what they care about, what questions they have, and how you can help.

Platform: Where does your target audience spend their time online? Is it Instagram, LinkedIn, YouTube, or somewhere else? And what can you say about viewer behavior on that platform?

Purpose: What's the end game? What do you want viewers to do, think, or feel after watching your video? Are you aiming for clicks, mindset shifts, or emotional connections?

Once you've got a handle on these 3Ps, you're well on your way to crafting videos with focus, videos that are created with your audience in mind.

With this foundation, let's see how you can use that to come up with fresh new video ideas.

And here's where AI comes in again! My first tries with using AI to get new video ideas were not very successful, though. It took quite a few mistakes and bad prompts to learn to write effective prompts.

HOW TO WRITE AN EFFECTIVE PROMPT TO GENERATE VIDEO IDEAS

How did your journey with AI start? You might have already experimented with ChatGPT. Ask it anything, and it instantly gives you answers.

For content creators, it can be incredibly useful for checking texts, crafting social captions, and translating texts, for example. But how do you craft a prompt that gives results you can actually use?

With AI, what you put in is what you get out. Do you put in a short, quick prompt? You'll get fast but not-so-thoughtful responses. But, if you share useful details in your prompt—about your audience, the platform, your previous videos, and your goals—then things get interesting. That's when ChatGPT delivers detailed answers that are much more targeted, giving you something you can really work with. Give more—and you'll get more back.

Let's put this into practice. You'll try out two different prompts. Prompt one: ask for a video idea around a certain topic: "Please give me ten video ideas for a dentist."

Prompt two: give ChatGPT info on your company before asking the same question. So, what kind of dentist is this? What makes it different from other dentists? And what is the goal for this video?

"I'm a local dentist in Delft, the Netherlands. We specialize in treating young children who are afraid to go to the dentist. Please give me ten ideas on videos on Instagram targeted to parents of young children."

YOUR AI SIDEKICK MIGHT NOT BE AS PERFECT AS YOU THINK

The more you use ChatGPT for video concepts, the more you'll stumble upon certain quirks and limitations. For example, if you ask ChatGPT for help with a hospital script, there's a good chance that every nurse mentioned will be female. And if you're brainstorming a video plan about a CEO, odds are ChatGPT assumes the CEO is a man. The more you use ChatGPT, the clearer it becomes that it sometimes struggles with adopting a feminist or non-Western perspective on topics.

According to researcher Daniel Hershcovich of UCPH's Department of Computer Science, "ChatGPT reveals in its responses that it is aligned with American culture and values, while rarely getting it right when it comes to the prevailing values held in other countries" ("ChatGPT Promotes American Norms and Values," 2023).

Source: "ChatGPT Promotes American Norms and Values." Department of Computer Science, University of Copenhagen, 2023, di.ku.dk/english/news/2023/ chatgpt-promotes-american-norms-and-values/.

Having ChatGPT on your video team is incredibly handy. The work ethic of this sidekick is off the charts. It's always there and ready to answer any question you throw at it.

But, this sidekick isn't always right, and the ideas it comes up with can be a tad outdated. While ChatGPT might be pretty skilled at using certain storytelling techniques, it doesn't inject a real human heart or genuine emotion into the stories it gives you.

THE THREE STEPS TO COME UP WITH NEW VIDEO CONCEPTS USING AI

ChatGPT is arguably the most well-known, but it's definitely not the only AI chat tool out there. Have you ever experimented with Google's Gemini? At first glance, it might look very similar to ChatGPT, but it uses different data sources. ChatGPT's data mainly comes from open web text, books, code, and Wikipedia. Gemini, on the other hand, mainly uses data from Google Search, Google Books, Wikipedia, and online dialogues.

Since ChatGPT and Gemini use different datasets, you could use each tool at different stages of your content creation process.

Here are three practical steps for brainstorming video concepts with the help of AI:

1. Research trends and existing competition with Gemini.

2. Transform video ideas into scripts with ChatGPT.

3. Finalize the script after a fact-check and add a human touch.

These steps are now an integral part of my video strategy approach at each company where I provide consultancy.

> No matter the company or its size, these three simple steps are an effective way to come up with creative business video ideas using AI. So, use them to your benefit!

These are the major phases of the process, but naturally, they involve a number of smaller steps. In the following paragraphs, you'll discover the smaller steps of each phase, complete with practical examples and exercises.

What's the difference between Gemini and ChatGPT for video creators coming up with video ideas?

Show drafts ⌄ ◀))

Here's a breakdown of how Gemini and ChatGPT might differ in helping video creators brainstorm video ideas:

Strengths:

- **Gemini:**
  - **Focus on Accuracy:** Since I prioritize factual accuracy, I can be a strong resource for informative videos. I can help research topics, debunk myths, and provide citations for credibility.
  - **Understanding of Search Trends:** I can tap into search data to identify trending topics and audience interests, giving you video ideas that are relevant and likely to get views.
- **ChatGPT:**
  - **Creative Spark:** ChatGPT is known for its creative text generation abilities. It might be better at coming up with unexpected or imaginative concepts for your videos.
  - **Engaging Scriptwriting:** It can help draft engaging scripts or storylines for your videos, potentially saving you time and effort.

Gemini explains the difference between ChatGPT and Gemini

Gemini vs. ChatGPT for Video Content Creators

Feature	Gemini	ChatGPT
Strengths	* SEO Optimization	* Conversational Fluency
	* Scriptwriting (including breakdowns & styles)	* Storytelling
	* Fact-Checking with Google Search Integration	* Content Translation

Export to Sheets

Gemini created a table of the different sources, strengths and weaknesses between ChatGPT and Gemini

If you're planning to use AI tools for creating videos for your business, there's something important you need to keep in mind. Some of these AI services might actually take the stuff you feed into them—like your ideas, scripts, or any data—and use it to make their systems smarter. This means your information could end up in their database, potentially exposed or used in ways you didn't intend. So, before using AI tools, make sure to check how they handle your data.

Look for clear privacy policies and ensure they're treating your information with the respect it deserves. It's all about keeping your data and ideas safe while still taking advantage of what AI can offer.

Also, it might be wise to draft an AI policy for your company. This can set clear guidelines on how AI tools should be used and ensure your team is on the same page about protecting your business's and customers' data.

1.Research.
Discover your target
audience & search
trends with Gemini

2. Video plan.
Come up with
a creative video plan
with ChatGPT

3. Human check.
Verify facts &
incorporate the
correct tone of voice

Three steps to come up with video ideas using AI tools

1. RESEARCH. DISCOVER YOUR TARGET AUDIENCE AND SEARCH TRENDS WITH GOOGLE'S GEMINI

Your first step: Google's Gemini. Why? Because Gemini is up to date on the latest trends on Google and YouTube, so it's perfect to generate new ideas that resonate with your audience.

Here's how it works: Give Gemini a detailed description on your target audience, including the hot topics, burning questions, or challenges they're facing. Then, ask Gemini for a list of twelve currently trending topics that will captivate your audience (make it twenty, ten, or three trending topics—whatever works for you!) Gemini not only gives you the trends, but you can also ask about the search volumes and competition levels per topic.

For example, when I was promoting my eCourse on Canva AI tools, I first did some research with Gemini on search volumes:

> *I'm developing an eCourse around AI tools in Canva. My audience is social media professionals, communication specialists, and business owners who create their own social media content. Can you give me an understanding of what people are searching on around Content Creation with Canva for social media? Please put the result in a table. Include search topics, search volume, competition, and amount of existing content.*

Topic	Search Volume (Google/YouTube)	Competition	Existing Content
Canva Social Media Creation: A Comprehensive Guide	8,000/40,000	Medium	High
Creating Videos with Canva: A Beginner's Guide	6,000/30,000	Low	Medium
Mastering Canva's AI Tools for Social Media Creation	4,000/20,000	Medium	Medium
Canva AI-Powered Video Creation: Tips and Tricks	3,000/15,000	Low	Low
Canva AI for Social Media: Enhancing Engagement and Reach	2,000/10,000	Medium	Medium
Canva AI for Social Media Content Creation Workflow	1,500/7,500	Low	Low
Canva AI for Social Media Marketing: Unlocking New Opportunities	1,000/5,000	Medium	Medium
Canva AI for Influencer Marketing: Building Stronger Connections	500/2,500	Low	Low
Canva AI for Social Media Analytics: Gaining Insights for Growth	300/1,500	Low	Low
Canva AI for Social Media Templates: Creating Eye-Catching Content	200/1,000	Low	Low

⊞ Export to Sheets

*Gemini can help you with search volume
and competition research*

After you have made a nice a list of relevant topics, Gemini can also help you discover what channels or creators are creating similar content.

> Just a year ago, I asked my wonderful intern to help me research a specific market, and it took her a full day to scour for competitors across all types of socials. But now, you can simply ask Gemini the question, and it will do the searching for you. This can save you a ton of time.

As you can see, there is a significant amount of interest in creating videos with Canva on both Google and YouTube. This suggests that there is a strong demand for information on how to use Canva to create high-quality videos.

Here are some of the most popular creators who create content on this topic:

- **Canva Academy** (Official Canva channel): This channel offers a variety of tutorials and guides on how to use Canva for different purposes, including creating videos.
- **Creative Cloud Tuts+** (Adobe's tutorial channel): This channel has several tutorials on how to use Canva to create videos, including motion graphics, intros, and outros.
- **Brandon Craft** (Social media marketing expert): This channel offers a variety of tips and tricks on how to use Canva to create effective social media videos.
- **Canva Masters** (Community of Canva experts): This channel has a variety of videos from different Canva experts on how to create videos with Canva.

By following the tips and using the resources from these creators, you can learn how to create high-quality videos with Canva and stand out from the competition.

*Gemini can help you research content
and similar content creators to you*

Gemini can give you a list of similar content creators. Then, you can simply check out their videos: scan their style, video duration, and personalities so you can think of ways to set yourself apart. You can also ask Gemini for personalized suggestions and specific things that work for your brand and audience.

Gemini can give you some great specific examples and tips for creating effective video content around your topic and brand. It can also give you ideas on different types of video formats.

> Time to try this out. Go to Gemini and give it a detailed description on your target audience, including your 3Ps you've already jotted down. Don't forget to also include your audience's current themes, frequently asked questions, and challenges they're facing. Then, tell Gemini you are looking for video ideas, and ask for a list of currently trending topics that might captivate your viewers.
>
> After that, continue the conversation with Gemini. Ask which topics are searched on often, which content creators make similar content, and work toward a list of video ideas until you've found some great ideas!

AI can help you track online behavior and engagement of your audience, analyze search intent and content preferences, identify emotion and tone that would work for your audience, and, last but not least, analyze video strategies from similar content creators. So, here are some questions to help you start your conversation with Gemini (or another AI tool!).

Questions to get to know your audience with Gemini:

Online Behavior:

- What websites, social media platforms, and online communities do my audience go to?
- What are their favorite brands, influencers, and content creators?

Search Intent:

- What are the top keywords and phrases that my audience is searching for on Google and YouTube?
- What is the intent behind these searches, such as information gathering, problem-solving, or entertainment?

- What type of video content does my audience prefer, such as educational tutorials, product demos, or behind-the-scenes glimpses?

Sentiment/Emotional Connection:

- What is the tone and sentiment of my audience's online conversations and reviews?

- What emotions do they express when discussing my industry or products?

Competitive Analysis:

- What videos are my competitors creating that are popular with my audience? What are the strengths and weaknesses of these videos in terms of content, production quality, and engagement?

- How can I differentiate my videos from my competitors and provide better value to my audience?

I've had the opportunity to train an incredibly diverse group of people in video creation—from total beginners to seasoned pros. This includes CEOs at multinational corporations, HR teams, managers, healthcare professionals, emergency responders, and interns. The goals might differ—some want in-depth interviews, while others want straightforward product videos—but they all have one thing in common: they want to reach an audience. They all want to make an impact. They want to create videos that make you stop scrolling and pay attention, videos that not only capture but also keep your focus. In a nutshell, they all want to get inside their viewers' heads and really understand what makes them tick.

2. VIDEOPLAN. COME UP WITH A CREATIVE VIDEOPLAN USING WITH CHATGPT

Your next step is to bring ChatGPT up to speed with the video topic, your target audience, current trends, and tone of voice/ type of video (such as video duration). Then, ask ChatGPT to put the video plan in a table with different columns for audio and video. You can also ask ChatGPT for ideas for an interesting start, to divide the video up in seven steps (use however many you think works for your topic), and an idea for the end of the video.

You

I'm about to create a video on how you can create videos with Canva: a beginners guide. This will be a step-by-step tutorial. Can you help me create a videoplan?
- Put the videoplan in a table, with different columns for audio (what is said), video (visuals), and timing.
- Please come up with an interesting start, a hook that will grab viewers attention.
- Divide the video up in 7 different steps.
- Give me examples of what I can say, how I can explain each step, and also fill in the column for visuals, give me examples of what I can show.
Give me an idea of how I can end the video. Please include a call to action to buy my eCourse 'Canva AI'

Before you answer, please ask me questions to create a better videoplan

An example of a conversation starter with ChatGPT.
Don't forget to tell ChatGPT to ask you questions

You probably ask ChatGPT questions. But does ChatGPT ever ask you questions? This one sentence in your prompt can help you get to your goal much faster: "Before you answer, please ask me questions."

Asking ChatGPT for questions can be very interesting because it often comes up with questions you hadn't thought of, such as: "How do you address your audience?" "Do you want to include humor?" or "Is this theme/question also relevant to your audience?"

ChatGPT will ask you for information that is necessary to craft the video plan you have in mind. The more information you give ChatGPT, the better it will be at crafting a video plan that works for your brand.

 **ChatGPT**

Certainly! Before we dive into creating the videoplan, let me ask you a few questions to better tailor the plan to your needs:

1. Who is your target audience for this Canva tutorial? Are they beginners with no prior design experience, or do they have some familiarity with graphic design tools?
2. Do you have any specific goals or key points you want to emphasize in the tutorial?
3. Are there any unique features or aspects of Canva AI that you want to highlight in your video?
4. What is the approximate length you are aiming for with this tutorial?
5. Can you provide some insights into the style and tone you want for your video? For example, is it more casual, professional, or a mix of both?

Once you provide these details, we can proceed to create a detailed videoplan that aligns with your goals and audience.

Tell ChatGPT to ask you questions to
get to an effective video format

The true power of ChatGPT is going back and forth: giving information, receiving back, then asking questions, getting answers, and so on. It's just like a real conversation and not a one-way monologue.

You

Thank you.

1. they are beginners with no design experience

2. I'd like to show how to create a basic video (slideshow, different shots after each other), but please also include how to add music, text and graphics or a logo to the video

3. Yes, please explain how you can change the timing of elements in your video

4. Between 7-10 minutes

5. It's casual, but for a professional audience. Jokes are welcome!

The best way to work with ChatGPT,
is a back-and-forth conversation

When you give ChatGPT more relevant information to work with, you are much more likely to get the result you are looking for. Asking the right questions and feeding the right info will lead to video plans with focus and clarity a lot faster.

ChatGPT

Great! With those details in mind, let's create a videoplan for your Canva tutorial. I'll structure it in a table with columns for audio, video, and timing.

Step	Audio (What is Said)	Video (Visuals)	Timing
1	**Introduction:** Start with an engaging hook. "Hey, aspiring video creators! Today, I'll show you how to turn your ideas into stunning videos using Canva, even if you've never edited before."	- B-roll of engaging Canva interface shots - Exciting background music	0:00-0:30
2	"Step 1: Setting Up Your Canva Account. If you don't have one yet, go to canva.com and sign up."	- Screen recording of the Canva signup process	0:31-1:00
3	"Step 2: Choosing a Video Template. Let's pick a template that suits your content."	- Navigate through Canva's template library - Demonstrate selecting a video template	1:01-2:00

↓

ChatGPT can create a videoplan for you in a table.
Ask for columns with audio, video, and timing

Go to ChatGPT, and first bring it up to date on your brand, your 3Ps, and the video idea you just came up with (with the help of Gemini). Then, ask ChatGPT to put the video plan in a table with different columns for audio and video. You can also ask ChatGPT for ideas for an interesting start, to divide the video up in different steps, and an idea for the end of the video. End the prompt with "Ask me questions before answering," and answer the questions ChatGPT gives you.

4	"Step 3: Adding Your Media. Upload your photos or videos to Canva for a personalized touch."	- Show the media upload process - Display examples of uploaded media	2:01-3:00
5	"Step 4: Customizing with Text and Graphics. Spice up your video by adding text, logos, or graphics."	- Illustrate adding text and graphics - Showcase a logo being incorporated	3:01-4:30
6	"Step 5: Setting the Right Timing. Control the pace of your video by adjusting the timing of elements."	- Guide on adjusting timing in Canva - Show before-and-after timing adjustments	4:31-6:00
7	"Step 6: Adding Music. Elevate your video with the perfect soundtrack. Canva has a library for you!"	- Demonstrate adding music - Briefly showcase Canva's music library	6:01-7:30

Use the table ChatGPT gives you as a foundation for your videoplan, then ask for changes as needed

This is how ChatGPT can save you a ton of time. It can help you divide your video up in different steps, give you ideas for visuals, and add a sense of the timing for the video.

If you want to pick from different types of scripts, you can ask ChatGPT for different video plan options and to make the tone of voice slightly different for each plan. In my case, though, the foundation was pretty good already!

If needed, you can continue the conversation with more questions. You can ask for a humor injection, out-of-the-box suggestions, a different tone of voice, or a few twists on the concept.

> Questions to help you in your conversation with ChatGPT:
>
> - What are some different ways to make this video visually appealing?
> - Can you make the tone of the script more conversational?
> - Can you add a joke or funny pun?
> - Can you come up with 5 different ways to start this video with an interesting hook?
> - Can you give me a shot list, interesting ways to film this video?
> - What are 3 ways to incorporate the call to action in a visual way?
> - Can you give me 3 places to add text or other graphics?

This is a process. Ask the right questions and feed the right info until you've crafted a plan that works best for your audience and your brand.

3. HUMAN CHECK. VERIFY FACTS AND APPLY THE RIGHT TONE OF VOICE

After you've created a video plan with the help of ChatGPT, it's time for a fact-check and human touch. While Gemini and ChatGPT are great at generating video ideas fast, they can still make mistakes. These tools help with ideas and a direction, but you should still be the expert steering the content. So, let's humanize what we've got!

> Let's put this into practice. It's time for the human check. Take a look at the video plan you have now. Are all the facts correct? Can you add your own thoughts, experiences, and words/visuals? Take out certain steps you don't think will be of interest to your viewers, change up the order of the steps if needed, and add your own stories and words—so you craft a plan that will resonate with your viewers.

Go through the script AI feeds you, and always double check the facts and information. Then, infuse the video plan with your unique insights, personal experiences, and human storytelling. This makes sure that you have a script that authentically connects with your audience.

A few questions for your human check:

- Is everything factually correct? Do you need an expert to double-check the facts and info?

- Does the order or storytelling make sense?

- Will your target audience stop scrolling if they see the start of the video?

- What will visually spark the interest of your viewers?

- What words will truly resonate with your audience?

- What tone of voice will work best for your viewers?

- Can you add any humor or emotional elements?

- What personal experiences or stories can you add to the script so it resonates with your viewers?

You know your audience best. So, add the words that resonate, the tone that speaks, and the visuals that truly captivate your viewers. This step is crucial in crafting a video that genuinely speaks to your viewers.

Now that you have an understanding of your audience, and you've crafted some video ideas for your brand, let's see if we can simplify the video creation process. More often than not, companies overcomplicate video formats . . . so, let's see if we can take the video ideas you have now, and simplify them!

2
SIMPLIFY YOUR BRAND VIDEOS: 3 LEVELS

You now should have some new video concepts laid out in front of you. Take a good look at them. How easy can you turn these ideas into actual videos?

Companies tend to make video formats complex, with a bunch of different shots and different interviews. While there's certainly nothing wrong with that approach, not every video needs to be that complicated, especially if your viewers are perfectly happy with a simpler format.

In this chapter, you'll explore whether you could simplify the video ideas you've come up with!

You're going to discover three levels of video creation, each with its own set of ideas, and you'll also get acquainted with some AI tools that can help you come up with fresh video concepts.

DOES YOUR VIEWER KNOW YOU?

The whole last chapter was all about knowing your audience. Now, let's flip it: does your audience know you?

As a content creator, you've got to always keep in mind where your viewers are at in their "customer journey." If they've just stumbled upon you while scrolling through LinkedIn or Instagram, they don't really know you yet and probably won't have much patience for your videos. They're likely not going to sit through minute-long videos, so it's a waste to pour tons of time into lengthy videos at this stage. So, if your viewers don't know and trust you yet, keep your videos short and sweet. Once you've built up some trust, you can often dive into longer, more insightful content.

Time for a little exercise. Does the viewer know you?

Where does your target audience fall in the customer journey:

- Viewers don't know you: Whip up simple, short social videos that grab your target audience's attention and introduce them to your brand.

- Viewers have heard of you/seen you: Create videos to build trust, like answering questions, showcasing your expertise, or busting myths.

- Viewers are about to take action: Craft videos to persuade. This is when viewers have the most patience for longer content (often on your website): product demos, FAQs, livestreams, interviews, testimonials, and so on.

- Viewers know and trust you: Make videos to keep in touch. You don't need to convince viewers anymore or win more trust, so simple is often best.

Once you've got a handle on where your viewer is in the customer journey, you might find you can simplify your videos.

HOW TO STOP OVERTHINKING YOUR VIDEO IDEAS

Getting tangled up in overthinking your video content? You're definitely not the only one. It's easy to make a video long, but it's tough to keep a video simple and short.

To streamline your brainstorming process and simplify your ideas, you can categorize videos into three levels:

Level 1. Single shot.

All you need is one well-planned shot, quickly filmed, and edited in a snap.

Level 2. Series of shots.

A slideshow of different shots put together. With a solid plan and some handy editing tools, you can make a level-two video in no time.

Level 3. Layered video.

This level usually involves interviews or presentations, supplemented with shots for visual explanation, which usually requires more time and attention for filming and editing.

LEVEL-ONE VIDEO: THE SINGLE SHOT SENSATION

Imagine you've got a new team member, and you want to create an introduction video. So, old habits might have you do a full on-camera interview with your new colleague, followed by some candid work shots, and maybe even some arrival-at-the-office footage. After filming the footage, adding graphics, music, and who knows what else, boom—you've clocked four hours on just this one video. But let's hit the brakes! Ask yourself: What are your viewers really here for?

SOMETIMES, ONE SHOT IS ENOUGH!

Sometimes, all you need is one clip—your new teammate in their new work environment, whether it's behind a desk, a machine, or working with a client. Throw in some text on screen, and voila! Done.

A level-one video doesn't need extra shots or require a ton of editing. It's quick to film, fast to edit, and guess what? Sometimes that's all your viewers want or need. They don't need a mini-documentary. They don't need to see that long interview or the whole process. Sometimes, just showing a single moment will do the trick.

The art of level-one videos is all about mastering the minimalist mindset. We're talking a snapshot of someone hard at work, a team member sharing a short golden nugget of wisdom, or just a quick shot of a product you love. These bite-sized videos are all over TikTok, Instagram Reels, and YouTube Shorts.

WHAT IF YOU ONLY HAD ONE SHOT?

Ever film yourself while working? It might sound a bit odd, but this is one of the simplest ways to make a level-one video. Pop your phone into a stand, or lean it against your laptop screen, and film away. Whether you're in a meeting, working on a project, typing an email, or chatting with a colleague.

You might think, "Who'd want to watch that?" But mix those clips with an interesting quote, a fun fact, or a Q&A, and you've got yourself short wisdom nuggets for your viewers.

Plus, these clips give your audience a behind-the-scenes look—they see you at work or home, interacting with someone else, hard at work (maybe amidst your kids' toys). Showing your viewers the real, unpolished you can add a layer of trustworthiness. And you'll find that these kinds of videos often draw a lot of viewers and interaction.

The best part about these level-one videos? They're super easy to make! You're already at work, your phone is right there, so why not film it?

Of course, this can apply to colleagues too. You can film your coworkers operating machinery, typing emails, grabbing coffee, working on a project, having lunch together, giving a presentation, and so on. The work's already happening; you just need to capture it. Follow a colleague for fifteen minutes during a workday, and you can easily film twenty usable shots for new videos. Just add some text and maybe some music, and your video is good to go!

10 IDEAS FOR LEVEL-ONE VIDEOS

Level-one videos aren't just great for promoting products or services; they're also perfect for sharing insights, celebrating small wins, increasing visibility, and building trust.

> No matter where you work, the type of company, or your brand goals, pretty much anyone can make level-one videos.

Here are ten ways you can use level-one videos:

1. **Daily Workspace Setup:**

   Capture a time-lapse of you or a colleague organizing the workspace in the morning.

2. **Quick Tip of the Day:**

   Close-up of a team member at work while sharing a valuable tip with text overlay for emphasis

3. **(New) Employee Introduction:**

   Brief intro of a (new) colleague in their workspace, with their name appearing on screen. This could easily be turned into a video series as well.

4.   **Favorite Work Tool:**

Have a colleague show and discuss their favorite work tool, on-screen text can explain why it's essential to them.

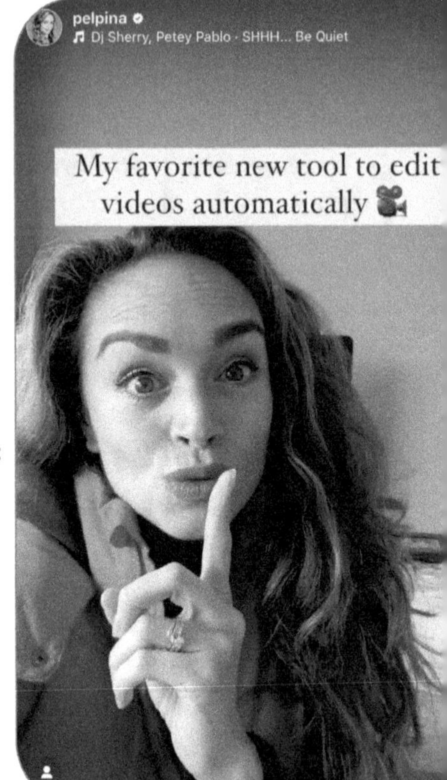

5.   **First Impressions Review:**

Film a teammate using/testing a new product. Text overlays can emphasize their initial thoughts and reactions.

6.   **Team Member's Favorite Book:**

Coworker holds up a book they recommend with a quick reason why it's a must-read.

7.   **Design Explained:**

Film a designer or engineer in your team briefly working on a new product's design or feature. Add text to underline the innovation and creativity involved.

8.   **Client Testimonial Snapshot:**

Short shot from a happy client, perhaps just a handshake with a colleague or simply waving at the camera. The text-overlay on screen can explain why they endorse your product or service.

9. **Product Packing Process:**

   A fast-forwarded video of a product being packaged
   and prepared for dispatch

10. **Upcoming Event Teaser:**

    One shot of the team in a meeting, a timelapse of the
    venue being prepared, or one shot of someone put-
    ting badges on tables; with overlay text announcing
    the date/time, for example

> It's time to see how you can use this within your own video strategy. Open Instagram or TikTok and see whether you can spot any level-one videos. How could level-one videos fit into your strategy? How can you simplify any current video ideas you have?
>
> What if you only had one clip, one shot, for your video—how would you do it?

LEVEL-TWO VIDEO: MULTI-SHOT IMPRESSION

Sometimes, one shot doesn't quite capture the whole story, especially if you're showing a process, highlighting different aspects of a product, or creating an event recap.

Capture the vibe with a collection of shots.

Say you want to capture the vibe of a typical day at work. One shot probably won't cut it. You'll need a variety of clips—meetings, interactive presentations, colleagues at work, and fun moments during coffee or lunch breaks.

For this level, you don't need to set up formal interviews in front of the camera. What you do need is short recordings of different moments to showcase the atmosphere. Put these shots over some music, and you've got yourself a vibrant impression.

And the best thing is you don't need sophisticated software to edit this type of video. With basic apps on your phone, you're set to go!

HOW TO CREATE CAPTIVATING LEVEL-TWO VIDEOS

Want to create a fun, engaging level-two video? It's all about mixing it up with your shots. In the next chapter, you'll discover much more on the art of dynamic filming. But for now, if you want to create a captivating level-two video, there are two key things to keep in mind while filming:

- **Play with angles and distances.** For example, when you're filming at an event, don't just focus on wide shots that show the size of the venue or the crowd. Also, film close-ups of attendees engaging in conversation, exchanging business cards, and jotting down notes. Put the camera high in the air, low on the floor, and film in slow motion and time-lapse; a mix of shots can help convey the vibe of the event.

- **Think about when to film.** What are the most important moments for filming? For example, at the event, what are the must-capture moments? When should you be ready and prepared to film? Pre-planning the "when" and "how" of your filming can make a huge difference in the outcome of a level-two video.z

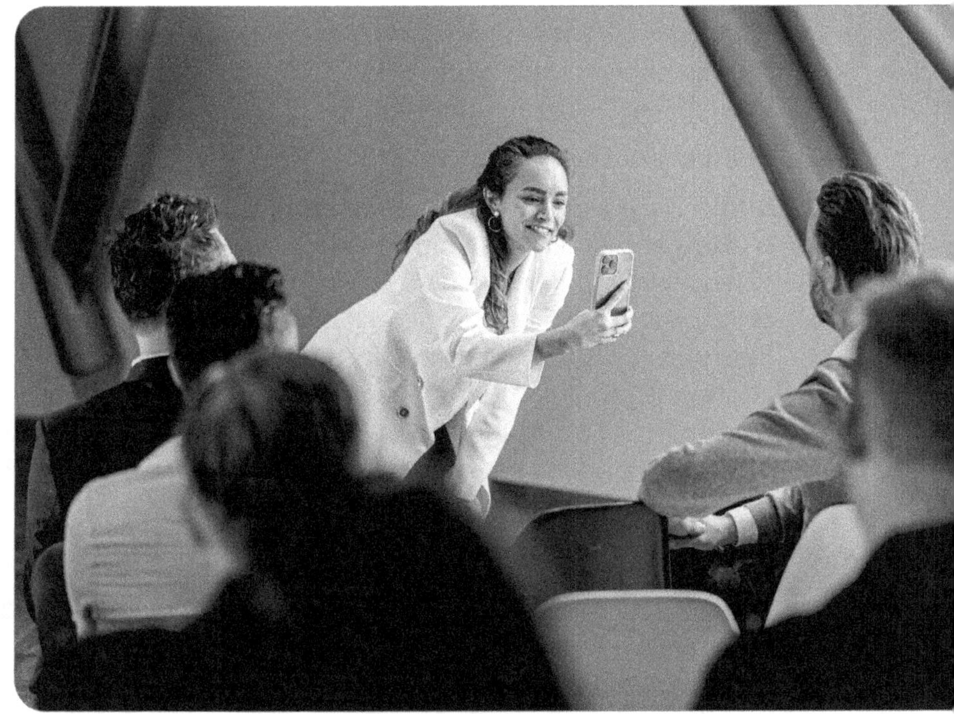

Rockateer / Bas Smeets

FAST EDITING OF YOUR LEVEL-TWO VIDEOS

Editing a level-two video can be very fast, but it really depends on what type of video you have in mind, as well as how much time and editing experience you have.

- **Editing with ready-made templates:**

  If you're short on time or not very experienced in editing, ready-made templates and AI editing tools are a lifesaver. For example, within Instagram and the CapCut app, you'll find loads of templates. These are premade editing projects, complete with music, transitions, and text—all you need to do is add your shots. You can have your video ready in no time.

  Quik by GoPro does something similar; this app picks the best parts of your recordings and syncs them perfectly with the music you choose. Then there's Canva, which has a "beat sync" tool—you add the clips, pick the music, and let Canva work its magic. You'll learn more about these tools later in the book.

- **Manual editing:**

   If you have a specific vision in mind, like each shot needing to be a certain length or specific music you want to use, you'll probably want to take control of the editing process yourself. Use the manual editing tools in apps like InShot, CapCut, or even Canva to manage the pace and duration of each shot. Keep in mind that editing manually will probably take longer.

> Time for a quick exercise! You're still brainstorming on video ideas, so why already think about editing tools? Well, the tool you choose for editing can change how you film and even impact your video plan.
>
> So, open Instagram or CapCut, find the editing templates, and scroll through them. In CapCut, you can also search for specific templates like "event recap" or "day in the life of" to see what pops up. What kind of videos do you come across? Which ones catch your eye? How could you apply these types of templates for your brand or business?

12 IDEAS FOR LEVEL-TWO VIDEOS

Level-two videos are ideal for impressions. Take your viewers on a day-in-the-life at work, show off a process with your coworkers, or capture the vibe of an event. Here are twelve examples of how you can use level-two videos:

1. **Process in Progress:** Film the step-by-step process of a routine task at your workplace, with close-ups and wide shots of each stage.

2. **First Day:** Document the first day of a new employee, capturing their introduction, workstation setup, team interactions, and first tasks.

3. **Guess the Colleague:** Create a playful mystery by showing close-ups of employees' desks, personal items, or even their pets, and let viewers guess whose space it is.

4. **Product Reveal:** Create a playful, engaging reveal of a new product, with fast cuts between its features, uses, and benefits.

5. **Emoji Day:** Film employees "describing" their day or a work task using only emojis (printed out or used in text on screen), followed by a few clips showing them engaged in the mentioned activity.

6. **Art of Crafting:** For businesses in crafts, showcase artisans working meticulously on products, highlighting their skills and the product's uniqueness.

7. **Good Morning Team:** Film different employees entering the building. How do they get in in the morning? Early, late, tired, excited? Still wearing workout clothes? Talking on the phone?

8. **Project Milestone Celebration:** Capture the joy and celebration of achieving a significant project milestone or goal.

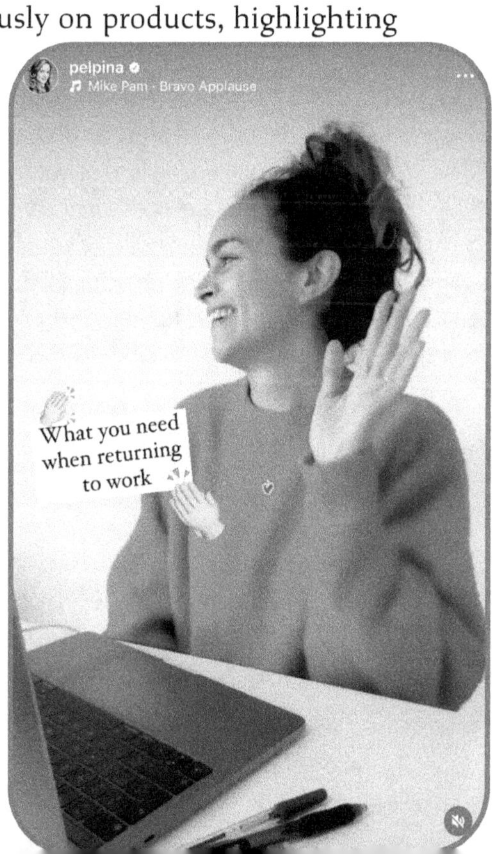

9. **Decor change:** Film the process of decorating and preparing the workplace for holidays, birthdays, or special work events.

10. **Superhero Alter Ego:** Colleagues reveal their "superpowers" used at work (typing champion, coffee barista?), with clips showing them in action, adding a layer of fun to everyday tasks.

11. **Workshop/Company/Studio Tour:** In just a few shots, give a dynamic tour of your workshop or studio, highlighting various areas, machinery, or tools and the work being done.

12. **Myth vs. Fact:** Are there any common misconceptions about your work or company? Film a few shots on the topic, and add texts debunking myths like "business videos take hours to make" with facts like "unless you smartly use your phone."

> Let's put to practice what you just learned. Take a look at your video plans or your current video strategy to see if there are videos that can be simplified into a level-two video. If you've already created a bunch of videos, review them. Which ones could you simplify? For which videos would level two have been just fine?

LEVEL-THREE VIDEO: VISUAL STORYTELLING

In video levels one and two, you've learned how to simplify your videos into single-shot videos or multi-shot impressions, but there are times when the story needs a bit more: a human touch, or someone in front of the camera explaining or sharing something. And that's exactly what a level-three video is all about! In a level-three video, there is one or more people speaking, complemented by the right visuals.

Level three is a bit more on the traditional side; it's usually what people think of when they hear the word "video." Think interviews, presentations, or showcasing new ideas and products, all accompanied by relevant visuals.

Show. Don't just tell.

Have you heard of "say dog, see dog?" It's a simple principle—what you hear is what you see. So, if you're talking about a dog, show a dog. If you're doing an interview about a product, then show the product. If someone's narrating a day at work, pair it with shots that match the story. This way, your video comes alive with visuals. It sounds simple, but there are still too many corporate videos that are just a "talking head," a person speaking with no accompanying visuals.

> Adding relevant visual shots hugely impacts how the video is received. So, before you start filming, prepare two things: what will be said, and what the viewer sees.

A-ROLL & B-ROLL

Back in the day, during the era of actual film, we used to handle an A-roll and a B-roll. These were basically two separate film layers that you would literally place on top of each other. I still remember my early days of film school at the University of North Texas, where we engaged in exercises cutting real film rolls. These days, fortunately, we don't need actual rolls—it's all a bit easier, but the basic principle and the terms still exist:

The A-roll serves as the main visual component in your video, often featuring key elements such as interviews, presentations, or vlogs. In the context of business videos, the A-roll typically centers around a person delivering information.

Say you're creating a video about a biking event, and you conduct an interview with a participant. In this scenario, the A-roll is the interview itself—quotes and insights from the cyclist about the event. The interview forms the backbone of your video, providing the essential narrative.

If you only rely on the A-roll, it would result in a video with just a talking head—in this case, the cyclist. If you want to add depth and context, you also need B-roll.

B-roll is the extra footage that complements the main narrative. For the video on the biking event, the B-roll would be shots of what the cyclist is talking about; shots of the start of the event, close-up of bikes, other cyclists in action, supporters chanting, and so on.

As you can see, level-three videos are a bit more complicated to make. That's why having a solid video plan becomes the cornerstone of bringing together the different layers. You need to prepare what's in the script (what's being said) and what you need to show (the shot list).

This is where a shot list come into play—a pre-determined list outlining all the shots you plan to capture. With this list, you can film with focus. And this saves you time during filming and editing.

WHEN SHOULD YOU MAKE A LEVEL-THREE VIDEO?

The power of a level-three video is in the human element—the person in front of the camera. These types of videos are perfect when your audience is ready for more in-depth content.

If your viewer is further along in the customer journey, say, they've already landed on your website, a more personal video with depth can build trust.

So, level-three videos are perfect for viewers who are looking for trust, testimonials, or want to see the product or service in action.

Keep in mind, though, that creating level-three videos takes some time. You have to set up an interview, gather the right quotes, and edit them down to just the right snippets. Then, you need to pair those quotes with visuals. But, if your viewers are looking for more in-depth videos, a personal connection, or a product or service in action, creating a level-three video is worth your time.

IDEAS FOR LEVEL-THREE VIDEOS

Level-three videos are where storytelling takes center stage. This is where you let people shine to get deeper connections with your target audience. They're perfect to shed light on the employee experience, showcase a day in your entrepreneurial journey, or unveil a new product. Here are some ideas to engage, connect, and convert with level-three videos:

1. **Customer Testimonials:** Film genuine feedback from happy customers, combined with shots of them using your product or service.

2. **Employee Spotlight:** Share stories of employees, their roles, and experiences in the company, showing them in their work environment.

3. **"Day in the Life" Vlog**: For entrepreneurs, showcase a typical day running your business with personal insights and behind-the-scenes shots.

4. **Expert Advice Series**: Regularly feature industry experts (could be team members) providing tips and advice, combined with relevant imagery and graphics.

5. **How It's Made**: Provide a step-by-step visual guide on creating your product with commentary from team members involved in each step.

6. **Industry Myth-Busting**: Experts in your team debunk common myths in your industry, supported by facts and graphics.

7. **"Before and After" Case Studies**: Visualize success stories of clients or projects with interviews and before-and-after imagery.

8. **Weekly Insights with . . .**: Have the someone on your team share weekly business insights or motivational messages with b-roll of the company in action.

9. **Customer Journey Explainer**: A satisfied customer narrates their journey with your company, supported by visuals of each stage.

10. **Trend Analysis**: Have an expert in your team analyze and discuss recent industry trends with appropriate visual aids.

> Now that you know what level-three videos all are about, it's brainstorming time. Grab a pen and paper, and start browsing through the video landscape in your industry. Go to LinkedIn, Instagram, YouTube, or whatever platform your target audience frequents. What types of level-three videos are your peers making? Absorb, analyze, and maybe even revisit some videos you've pieced together in the past. With a fresh perspective and the spark of ideas from the list we just explored, you might see new possibilities sprouting! Ready, set, brainstorm!

3.
SMART FILMING FOUNDATIONS: YOUR VITAL VIDEO CHECKS

Sometimes, you've got to make mistakes so you never make them again.

Summer 2009. I was about to interview one of my idols, an American tech celebrity: Shira Lazar. She had her own TV show, and I'd been following her for a while. After a lot of emails, I managed to arrange an interview with her for my video podcast: "WebBeat TV."

Of course, she didn't have much time; it would only last ten minutes. I was very nervous because it had to be done in one take, but the interview went well. Shira handled the conversation like a pro, and my nerves soon faded. It turned into a good conversation with some nice bits for my video podcast. Or so I thought.

After the interview, my editor walked up to me with a red face: "We have audio problems." Shira's sound kept cutting out during the conversation. We couldn't use large portions of the interview. Eventually, after a lot of tinkering, we managed to make a somewhat usable video podcast. But it still wasn't what it could have been.

And right then, I learned one of the biggest lessons in video making: Without audio, you don't have an interview. And without an interview, the foundation of your video crumbles.

Luckily, you don't have to make the same mistakes I did because in this chapter, you get all the basic checks for filming so you don't have to reshoot entire recordings!

For every video, whether it's an important interview with a CEO of an international company or a small vlog you're recording at home, always do a few simple, quick checks. Check your sound, the light, the background, and make sure your lens is clean.

In this chapter, you'll go through all the basic checks and receive practical tips. With these checks, you'll have a solid foundation to make brand videos like a pro.

AUDIO CHECK: HOW TO MAKE YOUR VIDEO SOUND LIKE A PRO

Did you know that good audio can instantly make your video look more professional? It's super important to dedicate some time and attention to this before you start shooting. Plus, you can't redo bad audio after an interview or vlog recording. Sure, there are (AI) filters to fix audio afterward, but you really don't want to rely on that. So, if you don't want to spend ages editing, make sure your audio is right during filming.

It all starts with being aware of the sounds around you while you're recording. Are you in a quiet hospital where people whisper and there's other distracting background noise? Or are you at an outdoor event with loud music? Or in a large industrial building with lots of echo?

A simple audio check usually takes a few seconds but can save you a lot of time in the edit.

Time for a quick exercise. Let's do a brief audio check right where you're reading this book:

- Close your eyes and be quiet for 5 seconds. What sounds do you hear?

- Say a few sentences. How does your voice sound in the room/space you're in?

- Take a look around you. Is there carpeting? Are there curtains? How is sound being reflected or absorbed in the room you're in?

When sound bounces off flat surfaces like windows, floors, or tables, it can create echoes. When sound is "absorbed" by fabrics or soft surfaces like carpets and blankets, it often results in a warmer sound. So, be mindful of the space and surroundings where you're filming.

Whenever I gear up for a video shoot, I often bring a few big blankets. These blankets have saved me multiple times by absorbing echoes in a room. I hang them up and drape them over flat surfaces like tables and floors. It might look a bit odd behind the scenes, but it makes the audio sound so much better!

HOW TO DO AN AUDIO CHECK IN 3 STEPS

Want to film like a pro? Then it's crucial to incorporate an audio check into your routine. It's not complicated, often takes less than a minute, and can save you a lot of editing time later on.

1. Head to the spot where you plan to record your video. Connect your microphone if you have one.

2. Record for about five to ten seconds. If the video includes dialogue, make sure the speaker(s) talk for a bit.

3. Play back the recording, preferably using over-ear-head-phones. Does the sound come through well?

If you don't have an external microphone and you notice too much background noise, try moving closer to the camera. And, always keep your ears peeled while recording because the sounds around you can change during filming. If a truck drives by or a gust of wind picks up suddenly, check the recording right away and redo it if necessary.

WHEN SHOULD YOU USE AN EXTERNAL MICROPHONE?

Sometimes, there's not much you can do about background noise. You can't always close all the windows or doors or ask your colleagues to be quiet.

That's where using an external microphone can be a game-changer. External mics are great at picking up voice sounds, even if you're at an event or recording on the beach with the wind blowing. There are tons of different microphones out there, and the best one for you depends on the kind of video you're making.

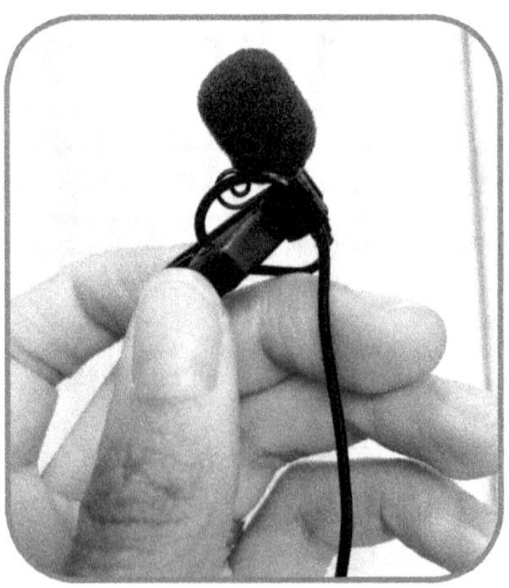

Clip-on (lavalier) microphone

CLIP-ON MIC: PERFECT FOR SOLO SHOTS

A lavalier, or clip-on, mic is perfect for videos where you're not moving around much and mainly have one person in the shot. There's a whole bunch of different brands and types of lavalier mics out there, from Sennheiser sets to the widely-used Røde Smartlav+ and the more affordable Boya lavalier mics.

HANDHELD MIC: GREAT FOR INTERVIEWS

For events or street interviews, a handheld mic can be a real asset. These mics focus the audio recording tightly on what's directly in front, cutting out a lot of background noise. But you do need to aim it properly at the person speaking.

WIRELESS MIC: FOR FLEXIBLE RECORDING

Don't like using cords? Go wireless with something like the DJI mic or Rode Wireless mics. These mics are pricier than most wired ones, but they're great for longer recordings (like following a colleague around the workplace with a camera), and they offer so much flexibility that you almost forget you're wearing them.

SHOTGUN MIC FOR "ON THE GO"

You simply attach this mic attach to your phone and aim at whatever or whoever you're filming. A shotgun mic is great for making "on the go" videos, moving around a lot, or doing spontaneous interviews with multiple people. Plus, neither you nor the person you're interviewing are tethered to your phone with a wire.

Reporter Microphone. Interviewing Jeremy Vest at Vidcon London, 2019

Before you buy a microphone, pay attention to these things:

- Is the microphone compatible with your smartphone? Double-check the description and connector.

- What kind of microphone are you looking for: lavalier, handheld, or a shotgun mic? What kind of videos will you mainly be making (interviews, vlogs, or event reports), and what kind of microphone is useful for that?

- Do you want a wired or wireless microphone?

- Does the microphone come with a windscreen?

- Can you use the microphone without having to download extra apps?

NO EXTERNAL MICROPHONE

You don't have to buy a microphone, of course; you can also just use your phone's microphone. One of the best-known innovators and inspirers in the field of mobile journalism is Yusuf Omar, who often doesn't use microphones or tripods. If you are not familiar with Yusuf's videos from @Seen.TV, definitely check them out. They're a great example that the quality of the story, your message, is what truly matters.

Yusuf Omar, multi-award-winning journalist and smartphone video expert

LIGHT CHECK: HOW TO LIGHT YOUR VIDEO LIKE A PRO

One of the best ways to make your video look more professional instantly: getting the lighting right. Simply shifting a bit or turning around in the room you're in can create a significant impact. This might sound easy, and it is, but you don't want to know how often it goes wrong. Many times, I come across videos where a slight tweak in the lighting angle could have vastly improved the overall visual appeal.

And just like with audio, light really needs to be done right while you're filming. Sure, you can edit it a bit afterward and throw on some filters, but trust me, if you've filmed harsh shadows on your face, you simply can't delete the shadows in the edit. Lighting needs to be right while you're filming.

GO FOR NATURAL LIGHT

The ideal lighting? Natural daylight. I've never met anyone who looks their best under harsh fluorescent office lights. While warm, yellow lights can create a cozy, romantic ambiance, they might not be the best choice for business videos.

So, if possible, and if it works for your video content, film in front of a window or consider filming outdoors. You've found a good recording spot, now pay close attention to the light. Where is it coming from? How does the sun's position relate to your subject?

Time for an exercise: a light check! Right where you are now, grab your phone, open the camera app, switch to selfie mode, and see how the light hits your face:

- Where's the light coming from? (Where's the sun/ where are the lights?)

- Walk around to see where the light best falls on your face.

- Move the camera up or down to see how it changes the light and shadows.

- How does the light hit your face? Can you see your eyes clearly? This is key: we connect through the eyes.

- Where are the shadows? Do the shadows improve if you stand somewhere else?

AVOID DIRECT SUNLIGHT

Filming in direct sunlight can be tricky. During a sunny and clear day, direct sunlight has the potential to cast harsh shadows on objects or faces.

If you're filming in broad daylight with the sun shining brightly, try seeking out indirect sunlight. That often means: move to the shade. Just look at the next pictures, both captured in the same spot, just a few meters apart.

Strong sunlight tends to create harsh shadows and make you squint

FILM DURING THE GOLDEN HOUR

Have you heard of the golden hour? Every photographer or videographer is familiar with it. The golden hour is in the early morning or early night, when the sun rises or sets, and everything around you gets a nice golden glow. Shadows become less harsh. It can create beautiful, soft lighting and nice warm colors. With this in mind, you could plan your video shoot around the golden hour, especially if you're looking for nice fill shots of landscapes or nature.

Same spot, different light. The golden hour can create a nice golden glow, soft shadows, and warm colors

HOW TO ENSURE GOOD LIGHT WHEN FILMING INDOORS

If you're going to film indoors at a location you haven't been before, it might be a good idea to check it out in person beforehand. Or, if that's not possible, ask for some photos or videos of the location. Then, you'll know in advance if there are a lot of windows, mainly fluorescent lights, curtains, and so on. This way, you get familiar with the lighting situation ahead of time and can prepare accordingly.

It's more than just standing in front of a window.

If you're filming indoors, find the best window and stand in front of it. You probably knew this already. But what you might not yet apply is the fact that good lighting changes throughout the day. If you have perfect light at a certain window in the morning, by the afternoon, you might often find yourself moving your video gear—just because the light hits differently.

I usually film at the front of our house in the mornings and often move my video shoot to the back of the house in the afternoons—I essentially follow the sun.

So, always check the lighting conditions before you record. And a golden rule: never stand with your back to a window or light source, or you'll turn into a dark silhouette. Make sure the light hits your face. Just take a look at the shots below, taken at the same window, just from a slightly different angle:

Same window, same spot, different angle!

WHEN SHOULD YOU USE ARTIFICIAL LIGHTS?

If it's impossible or impractical to film near a window, or if you do a lot of filming in the evening, you might want to work with artificial lighting. Continuous lights are the best choice for video, and there are several options to choose from, depending on what type of videos you make.

LED Lighting: Often filming on the go? LED lights might be just what you need. They're compact, lightweight, and provide beautiful illumination. Most LED lights run on mains power, which is great for indoor filming. But if you want to avoid the hassle of cords and extension cables, consider battery-operated LED lights.

Softboxes: Softboxes mimic natural light beautifully because they provide nice, even lighting. The biggest downside is that they take up more space and can be a bit of a hassle to assemble or disassemble for each shoot. They're particularly useful for a permanent filming location.

Construction Lights: Looking for a simple DIY solution? Use a work light! Reflect the light from a work light off a white wall or ceiling for indirect lighting. But be careful; construction lights can get very hot, so don't place anything too close.

LED lights: Do most of your videos take place in different locations? Then LED lights might be a good solution for you. They're small, light, and produce nice lighting. A lot of LED lights have a wire. So, if you want to be extra flexible about where you shoot, buy battery-powered LED lights.

Softboxes: These lights mimic natural lighting very well; they create nice, even lighting. The biggest downside to these lights is that they take up more space, and that it's a bit of work to put them together/take them apart for every shoot. So, softboxes are mainly useful for a fixed shooting location.

*Filming
with softboxes*

*my sister
Joseffa filming
with softboxes*

HOW DO YOU GET RID OF SHADOWS
WHEN YOU WORK WITH ARTIFICIAL LIGHTS?

Once you start working with artificial lights, you'll probably notice shadows popping up. And if you don't know how to light a subject properly, it can be super frustrating trying to get rid of shadows.

- The best way to light a subject is using three-point lighting. It's a technique often used in photography, videography, and film. The concept is simple: Light a subject from three different angles with three sources of light. **Key Light:** Place the brightest light at an angle in front of the subject.

- **Fill Light:** Notice shadows on one side? Position the fill light to soften or fill those shadows.

- **Back Light:** Your back light goes above or behind the subject, helping to separate them from the background and eliminate shadows on the backside.

Host and producer Gary Leland using 3-point-lighting

"I have attended events where I actually took an entire suitcase full of video gear. Because of my iPhone, I can now carry all my gear in a small camera bag. I love using my iPhone to shoot my video and use it every day to do so."

—Gary Leland, host and producer
of The Four Minute Crypto Show
and the Fastpitch Softtball TV show

You definitely don't need three lights for every shoot. But, if you're wondering why you keep seeing shadows while filming, then these techniques are worth applying. They'll help you avoid unwanted shadows and make your subject stand out from the background.

> For most video shoots, just remember to use daylight when possible, and if you're shooting inside and are using artificial lights, use white continuous lights.

HOW TO MANUALLY CHANGE THE EXPOSURE ON YOUR PHONE

Ever tried filming someone, only to find the background was beautifully lit, but the person was way too dark? Or the opposite: the background was too bright? The best way to avoid these issues is by manually changing the exposure on your phone.

> Time to try this out. Let's adjust the exposure on your phone. Open your camera app and pick an object to film. Now, simply tap the object on your screen. On most phones, you'll see a yellow or white circle or square appear around the object. Now, try tapping the background. This will bring the background into focus and adjust the exposure accordingly.

If you're standing in front of the camera, just tap on your eyes. If you're filming a landscape, you can tap on different areas (the tree in the foreground, the grass in the background, or maybe the sky). You'll see that the phone then adjusts and optimizes the exposure based on the distance you choose.

Tap your screen to change the focus and light

HOW TO MAKE THE WHOLE SCENE BRIGHTER/DARKER

You can manually adjust the lighting on your smartphone. On iPhones, after tapping the screen, you can move the yellow sun icon up or down. On most Android phones, you can move a lamp icon or a + or – to make your entire image brighter or darker.

Move the sun (iPhone) or lightbulb (Android) to adjust the lighting

HOW TO LOCK THE EXPOSURE AND FOCUS

Want to keep the exposure and focus the same throughout the recording? Press and hold on the spot you want well-lit and in focus for two seconds. For example, tap and hold the screen right at the eyes when you're filming someone. You'll see a notification that says "AE/AF Lock" or "locked."

Now you've locked the light and focus. It doesn't matter if you move the camera, the light/focus settings will stay the same throughout the recording.

To unlock, just tap another part of the screen. Keep in mind this feature varies by phone; it may not work on every device, and on some phones, it only works using the rear camera.

Hold your finger in place for two seconds to lock the exposure and focus (works on most phones)

If you want more control over the exposure, check out the FilmicPro app. This paid app gives you much more control over the exposure than most camera apps. With Filmic Pro, for example, you can set the exposure and focus separately.

WHAT IF THE COLORS LOOK WEIRD?

Your smartphone automatically handles white balance for you. And in most cases, it gets it perfectly right, and you don't have to worry about colors looking off. But if you notice your shots look too blue or too orange, it might be a white balance issue.

To understand how white balance works, you need to know a bit about color temperatures. All light sources have a color temperature (measured in Kelvin, thanks to the brilliant scientist who came up with this system). For every situation—whether it's daylight in the sun, indoors at the office, or outside in the shade of a tree—color has a different temperature. Colors with a temperature close to direct sunlight appear white, lower temperatures have a red/yellow tint, and high color temperatures look more blue/green.

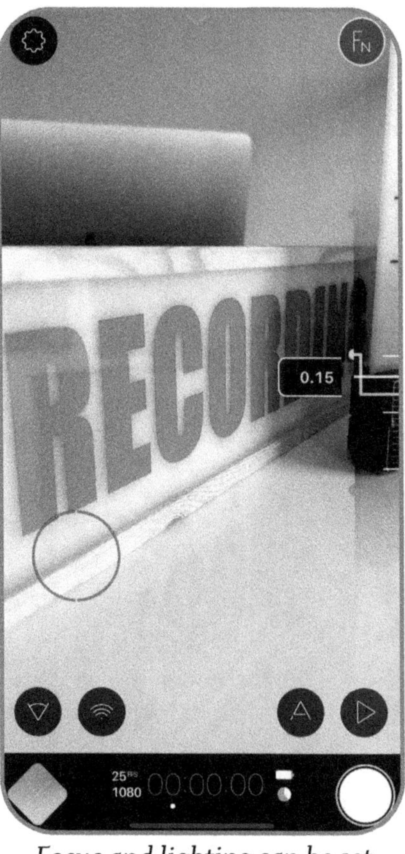

Focus and lighting can be set separately in the app Filmic Pro

So, colors look different in every situation, and your phone's camera tries to capture colors as accurately as possible based on the scenario. Usually, it does a pretty good job, but if you find the colors are more yellow or blue than in reality, you can tweak this.

> With white balance, you are telling your camera what is white: which color is neutral. Based on that white color, the camera can figure out how other colors in your scene should look.

Usually, showing your camera something white (like a T-shirt or a piece of white paper) is enough. The camera often adjusts the colors automatically. Most phones also have different lighting settings (sunny, cloudy, indoor) you can use. And if you want to perform a manual white balance, there

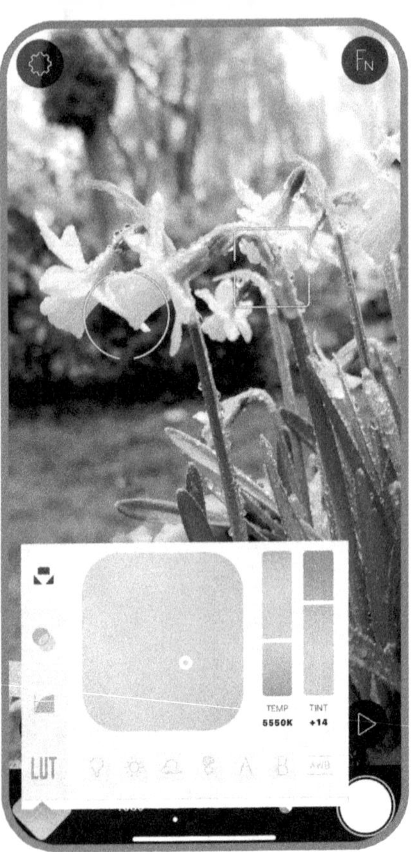

*Change the white balance
with the app Filmic Pro*

are various white balance apps out there, like "Filmic Pro."

Noticed the colors are off after you've filmed? You can adjust the colors afterward straight from your gallery or camera roll on most phones (so you don't need an app). Simply open the video and go to "edit." On most phones, you'll find a bunch of options to adjust colors, saturation, and exposure. It's great to tweak the colors after you've filmed!

Time to grab your phone and discover how to edit your videos without opening an app. Open a video in your camera roll or gallery on your phone and tap "edit" (or look for something similar). You'll then see different options to edit your selected video.

Often, you can adjust the colors, saturation, and brightness. And on many phones, you can mirror, rotate, and even trim your video. Take a look at what editing options you have on your phone. For many people, this is quite the revelation!

CAMERA CHECK: FRAMING LIKE A PRO

Now that you've checked your audio and sorted out your lighting, it's time to move on to the next check: stabilizing and framing. Are you holding your phone yourself? Or are you going for a tripod or stabilizer? And how far away should you put the camera?

HANDHELD FOR INFORMAL VIDEOS

Handheld filming can be great for some purposes. Vlogs, Instagram Stories, and behind-the-scenes videos can be perfect to film by hand. Of course, the video might be a bit shaky, you always have one hand occupied, and you can't stand too far from the camera. But these elements can create an informal, personal, casual atmosphere you might be looking for.

Handheld interviewing on the go:
fast, simple, and spontaneous!

EVERYTHING IS A PHONE HOLDER

Your phone is compact, light, and can pretty much stand anywhere. Pop it on a shelf on the wall or outside against a tree. Want to film yourself cooking? Tuck your phone into a kitchen cabinet above you, with the camera pointing down. And if you're filming yourself at the office, you can simply lean your phone against your laptop screen.

If you take a good look around, you'll find spots everywhere where you can place or lean your phone. This way, you can film yourself with a steady shot while keeping your hands free.

MINI TRIPOD FOR VIDEOS ON THE GO

Even better than scouting spots to place your phone? Having a phone holder with you. A mini tripod takes up little space in your bag and often comes in handy.

The Benro BK10 is a selfie stick that can also function as a tabletop tripod. With this small tripod, you can film yourself at the right height, you have your hands free to demonstrate something, and you can stand however far away from the camera you want.

Using the Benro BK10: a selfie-stick and tripod in one

STABLE FILMING WITH EYE-LEVEL TRIPOD

A standard tripod offers flexibility in positioning your phone. It's useful to have a tripod that allows you to film at least at eye level and has a built-in leveler. And, of course, make sure you have a smartphone holder for use with the tripod.

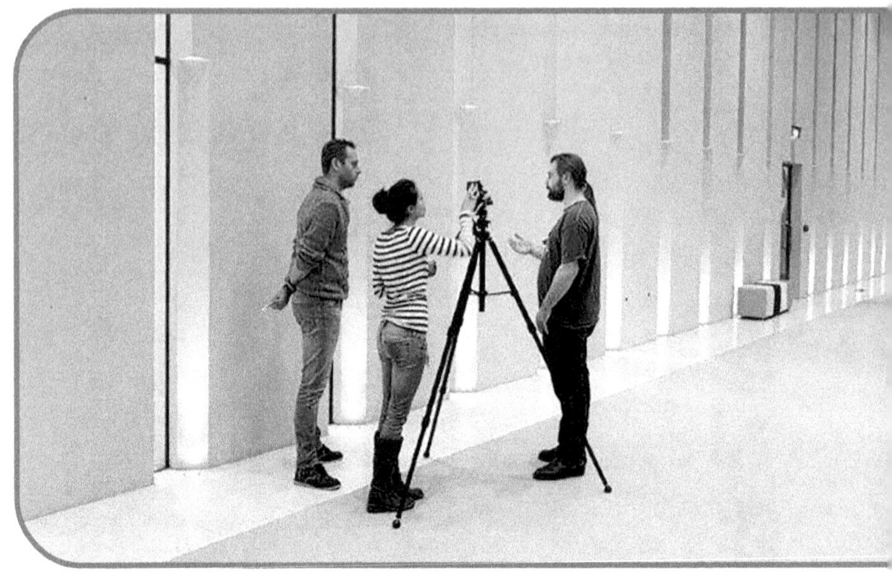

Interviewing with the tripod at the Dutch Forensic Institute

When purchasing a tripod:

- Verify the maximum height to ensure you can film and interview at eye level.

- Check if the phone holder fits (the width of) your specific phone.

- If you want to easily switch between horizontal and vertical shots, take a look at the holders from Joby and Manfrotto for smartphones.

- Check the weight of the tripod. If you're filming in different locations; you'll be carrying your tripod around a lot. Lighter is better.

- On a tight budget? Then a light stand might be worth considering. It gets tall and is foldable and lightweight. Downsides: you can't adjust the height per leg, and there's no built-in bubble level.

STABILIZER FOR A SMOOTH RIDE & SOLO FILMING

If you're capturing a lot of action shots on the go, a mobile stabilizer, or gimbal, can be a lifesaver. It ensures your shot is steady, even when your hands are shaky or if you move around a lot. Many phones nowadays have a built-in action mode that can also provide a steadier shot. But, there are phone gimbals, which, aside from stabilization, offer more cool features.

With DJI's mobile stabilizers, for example, you can seamlessly switch between horizontal and vertical modes. This lets you transition from vertical shots for your social media content to landscape shots for your web-site—with just one button. Plus, this stabilizer also has a "face tracking" mode: it follows the person in front of the camera. This can make it seem like someone is operating the camera, even when you're filming solo!

"If I'm creating quick content, I like to use my iPhone. I carry a mini tripod, LED lights, and Rode microphones to be able to film videos or livestream on the go."

—Goldie Chan, LinkedIn Expert & Video Content Creator

SHOULD YOUR VIDEO BE LANDSCAPE, PORTRAIT OR SQUARE?

Do you film horizontally (landscape) or vertically (portrait)? The quick, simple answer: look at your audience. Is your audience watching on a phone? Then film vertically. Are they on a laptop or desktop? Then go with horizontal. But it's not always that simple, unfortunately.

> Whether your video should be horizontal, square, or vertical also depends on the platform where you're posting it. And social platforms like LinkedIn, Instagram, Facebook, and TikTok are always changing.

For years, the standard format on TikTok, for example, has been vertical. But in January 2024, news broke that TikTok was starting to support horizontal videos too. We've yet to see how this will play out, but it perfectly illustrates how the video landscape is constantly evolving. So, keep up-to-date with the current norms on your chosen platform.

WHEN SHOULD YOU FILM LANDSCAPE?

Landscape videos work well for larger screens, like laptops, TVs, and desktops. Film landscape (horizontally) if:

- Your audience primarily watches videos on desktop/laptop.
- The videos are posted on Vimeo, a newsletter, your own Video Management System, or another system that mainly supports landscape videos.
- The videos are used in presentations, at events, or on other large screens.
- If you're unsure whether to film vertically or horizontally, it's smart to opt for horizontal. You can easily crop horizontal footage to square or vertical with various tools, but it's often harder to do the reverse.

WHEN SHOULD YOU FILM PORTRAIT?

Portrait (vertical) videos are a must on TikTok, Instagram, and YouTube shorts, as these videos are mostly viewed on phones. Film vertically if:

- Your audience primarily watches social videos on mobile devices.

- Your videos are mainly made for TikTok, Instagram, Snapchat, YouTube shorts, or other vertical-first platforms.

WHEN DO YOU MAKE YOUR VIDEO SQUARE OR ANOTHER SIZE?

Almost all social networks also support square videos. And it's no wonder: square videos (1:1) get more engagement and views than landscape videos, mainly because they take up 78 percent more of a phone screen than landscape videos do. Plus, square videos are always displayed in the correct format, regardless of whether the viewer holds their phone vertically or horizontally.

The biggest downside of square video? Most smartphones can't film in square format. So if you're recording a video with the goal of making it square, remember that parts of the canvas will be cut off.

> If you want to ensure everything fits into the square video, here's a tip: cover the screen with tape/paper until you have your 1:1 screen.

Another popular format for socials is 4:5, making your canvas slightly taller than it is wide. If your phone doesn't film square or 4:5, you can use apps like Filmic Pro and Clips to film in these formats. Or, you can crop your video after filming—simply from your camera roll or with apps like InShot or Capcut.

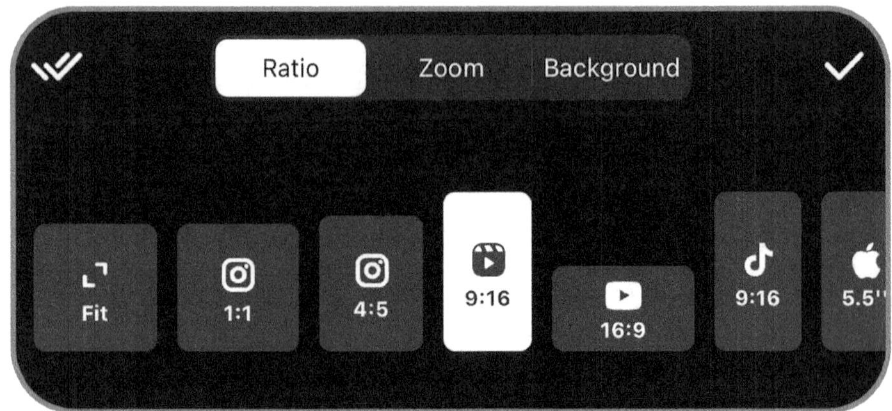

Change the canvas size with the app InShot

WHEN'S THE LAST TIME YOU CLEANED YOUR CAMERA LENS?

Let's talk about something tiny that can make a huge difference in how professional your video looks: your lens. When was the last time you cleaned it?

"I have a really bad camera, just look." During my video workshops, it happens often that someone comes up to me showing "bad" footage, totally convinced their camera is at fault. But more often than not, it's not a bad camera; it's a dirty lens. It's crazy how a little smudge can make such a big difference. So, before you go out and buy a new phone, give your lens a clean!

Imagine you've nailed all the other checks—your sound is crystal clear, your composition is on point, and the lighting is just right. If your lens is dirty, none of that matters. That tiny speck or dust on your lens can make your whole video look less professional. And remember, you can't clean your lens in post-production. So, do you want sharp, clear shots like a pro? Make sure your lens is clean.

ENSURE FOCUS DURING YOUR SHOOT
BY SWITCHING THIS ONE BUTTON

Imagine you've scheduled an important video interview. Setting it up took quite a bit of planning and coordination, and you only have fifteen minutes to interview the person. So, you put your phone in place, test the microphone, hit record, and the conversation starts. The interview goes smoothly until . . . your phone rings. You get a call. And the recording abruptly stops. Now, the focus is gone, and you have to start over.

This is why there's one button you'll want to switch on before starting any important recordings: The "Do Not Disturb" mode. This mode ensures you're not interrupted by calls, messages, or other notifications. On many phones, an incoming call stops the recording. And that's probably the last thing you want.

Time for a quick exercise. You might have guessed it: if you don't know how to set your phone to "Do Not Disturb," now's the time to find out.

On most Samsung and iPhone phones, you swipe from the top to see your quick menu. From there, you can often enable the "Do Not Disturb" or "do not disturb" mode. However, its location varies slightly on different phones. So, if you're not sure how to activate "Do Not Disturb" mode on your phone, take this as a sign to check Google. It'll take a couple of minutes now, but it'll give you peace and focus while filming later.

VIDEO SHOOT CHECKLIST

PREPARATION

◯ Define 3P's: People, platform, purpose
◯ Create a videoplan/script + a shotlist
◯ Prepare shoot (arrange location/interview/props)
◯ Check: can you film multiple videos at once?

BEFORE FILMING

◯ Light check: Find the best spot with good light and/or add lights
◯ Audio check: Find the best spot for good audio and/or test mic
◯ Framing: decide whether you'll film landscape or vertical
◯ Background check: make sure the background is ok
◯ Text/logo placement: make sure there is space for text/logo/etc
◯ Clean your lens
◯ Put your phone in airplane or 'do not disturb' mode
◯ Notes: Grab pen/paper to jot down timecodes, quotes & shots

AFTER FILMING

◯ Delete shots you won't need
◯ Put the best shots in a separate folder
◯ Write down notes immediately about timecodes, quotes,
shots & order to edit faster

7X AI TECH BUILT INTO SMARTPHONE CAMERAS

Did you know there's a pretty good chance your phone already has some form of AI technology built into it? Many modern smartphones have so much AI tech baked in that we often don't even realize we're using it. And guess what? There's a lot more on the way!

1. Automated Framing and Composition:

    Google Camera, on Pixel phones, uses AI to suggest the best framing and composition for shots. It does a scene analysis for you, and the app suggests adjustments to capture subjects in the best possible way so it can help you create well-balanced and visually appealing shots.

2. Auto-Focus and Tracking:

    Many smartphones, including those with Dual Pixel Autofocus technology, use AI for advanced auto-focus and tracking things in your frame. So, if you film a lot of action on the go, this technology helps with smooth and precise focus adjustments so your subjects remain sharp and in focus!

3. Gesture and Voice Commands:

    Google's Camera app uses AI technology for gesture controls, so you can capture photos or start a video with simple hand gestures. It's great if you want to create a hands-free video or picture!

4. Intelligent Lighting Recommendations:

    Samsung's Camera app uses AI through its Scene Optimizer feature. It recognizes various scenes and adjusts your camera settings automatically. It can even optimize lighting conditions for better exposure. How neat!

5. Scene Recognition for Scene-Specific Settings:

    Certain Huawei smartphones have an AI-driven camera system with scene recognition. The AI analyzes scenes in real-time, identifying specific settings and adjusting camera parameters to enhance image quality, all automatically!

6. Dynamic Depth of Field Adjustment:

    Many smartphones feature Portrait mode or Cinematic mode. They use AI technology to dynamically adjust the depth of field. This lets you capture photos and videos with a blurred background and also allows you to adjust the depth of field after recording.

7. Real-time Feedback on Shot Quality:

    This isn't AI technology integrated into the smartphone but an app definitely worth a mention. The Open Camera app gives real-time exposure feedback using AI algorithms. This app can give you instant information on your shot quality, including exposure levels, enabling adjustments on the fly for optimal results.

4
FRESH FILM
TECHNIQUES FOR
CAPTIVATING
SOCIAL VIDEOS

Ever filmed something so boring you almost dozed off yourself? Predictable meetings, lifeless offices, never-ending events … You might think: this is so dull, so mind-numbing—there's no way to make a fresh, dynamic video out of this.

> "You taught me to see the world differently" is one of the nicest compliments my students can give me after a video workshop. I believe there's no such thing as a boring subject—just a boring way of filming it.

In this chapter, you're going to discover it's not what you film but how you film it. You'll learn how to add movement to your videos, explore different ways to engage your audience from the start, and get acquainted with cool transitions.

It's not about the subject; it's about you, the videographer, looking at your surroundings differently. Learning to capture movement and film from various perspectives makes telling a dynamic story second nature. And that's the best way to grab your viewer's attention.

MAKE YOUR VIDEOS DYNAMIC BY CHANGING PERSPECTIVES

Most people film the same way. They grab their phone, hold it at their eye level, and start recording. Just take a look at people filming a game on a soccer field or during a concert: all the cameras are at the same height. And that's natural, of course, because you film how you're used to seeing the world.

> Let's do another quick exercise. Grab a nearby object. It doesn't matter what it is—a pen, a cup, a set of keys, or this book.
>
> - Film three short shots of your object.
>
> - Review your shots. Did you place the camera at your own eye level, or did you experiment with height?
>
> - Watch your shots again. Is there movement in the shots? For example, did you write with the pen or flip through the book? Or, was the movement not in front of the camera, but did you move the camera itself?

You're used to viewing the world around you in a certain way. You perceive at a certain height, with a certain pace, and with certain colors. So, it's not strange that you tend to film in this way as well.

However, if you're looking for dynamic, different, fresh shots that grab your viewer's attention, try aiming for surprising angles, heights, perspectives, and speeds. Film in ways your eyes aren't used to seeing.

FLIP YOUR PHONE

Ever filmed with your phone upside down? Placing the bottom of your phone on the ground or a table gives you a totally different perspective. With this technique, you can create awesome cooking and food shots but also unexpectedly fun shots of a meeting around a table, for example.

FLY FROM ABOVE

You can also hold your phone up high, with the camera lens facing down. Your camera lens looks from top to bottom at the subject, also known as a bird's-eye view. Don't have a long selfie stick? Simply tape your phone to the ceiling, and this, too, guarantees an unexpected shot!

UP CLOSE AND PERSONAL

Super close-ups can reveal intrinsic details you don't normally see; a super close-up of writing on a whiteboard, for example, is so close that you can see the ink appearing on the board or small details that set the atmosphere of an event, like a super close-up of champagne bubbles or a handmade thank-you note.

Filming a product from above, with the Benro BK10 Tripod

To get sharp super-close-up shots, film in macro mode, or try using the ultra-wide lens on your phone and get very close up to the object you're filming.

WIDE SHOT

How about a shot from afar after that close-up? A total shot of a large event hall or a wide shot of the office, for example, can add context. It shows the viewer where you are. The wide-angle lens is perfect for this, showing more of the surroundings.

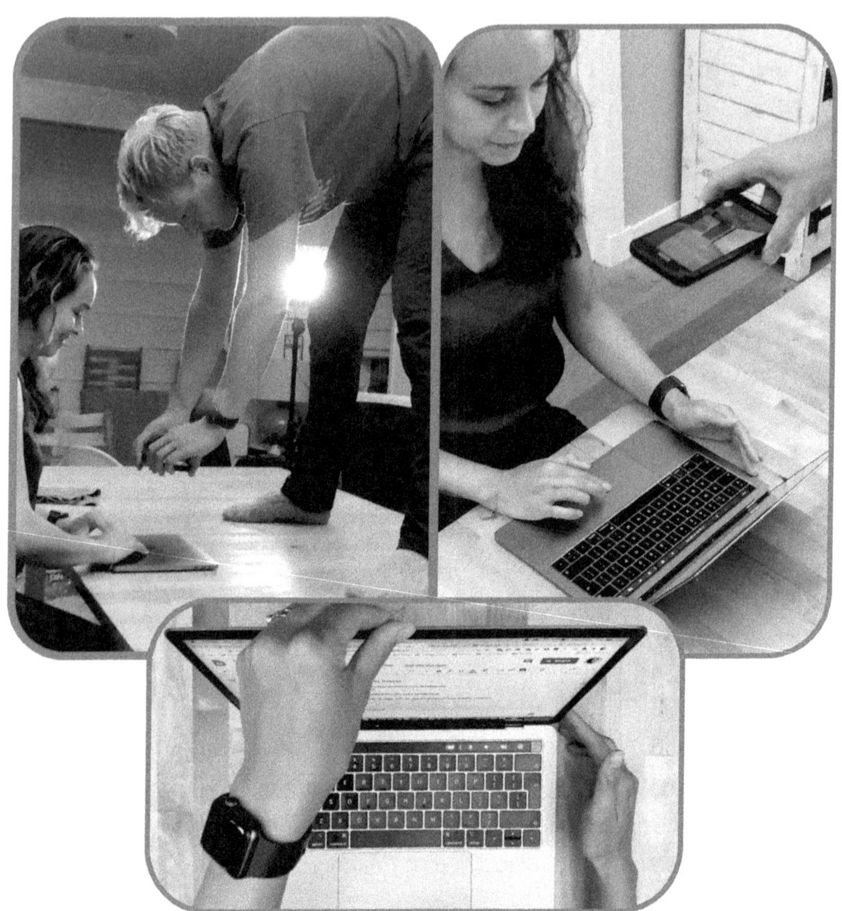

*Film from different angles and distances to
create captivating shots*

Looking for some creative inspiration? Try taking at least five shots from different angles and different distances. Start with one shot and then change the distance (further away or closer), but also the angle (from above, below, oblique, filming through something). This forces you to think differently and often leads to other, more creative, shots.

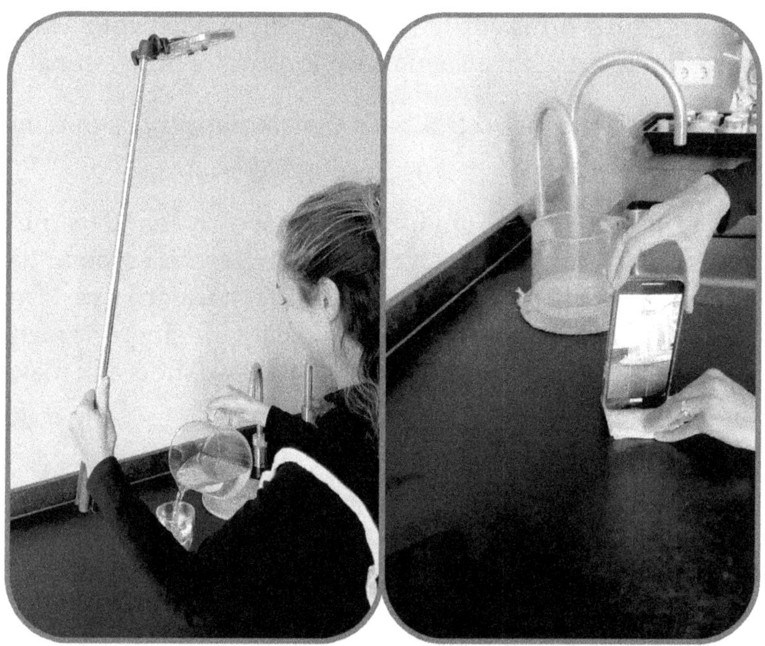

Filming from a low angle, from above, and through glass

USE THE DIFFERENT LENSES ON YOUR PHONE

Turn your phone around. How many lenses do you have? With different lenses, you can capture different kinds of shots. I most often film with my regular lens, use my wide-angle lens to capture big scenes, and the close-up lens for more detailed shots. So, when you're setting up the beginning of your video, don't forget to swipe between lenses to see which one works best.

The wide-angle lens is perfect to show a big view and show your surroundings. But, when you want to focus on small things, like details of a product, the close-up lens is perfect. Interestingly, using the super-wide lens to film super close-up can also result in unexpectedly fun shots.

Filming with different lenses not only makes your video more interesting but also makes it look more professional.

Quick question for you: What's the element that's missing from all these shots?

You've ventured through different perspectives and learned how to film from up close, above, below—you name it. It's already a significant change from the standard eye-level viewpoint. But, there's one big thing that's missing, one main ingredient that will completely change these shots and make them a lot more dynamic.

Can you guess what I'm talking about . . .?

MOVEMENT.

> A video can come alive through movement in your shots. Without any form of action, it's essentially a still image. Something needs to happen to capture and maintain the viewer's attention.

HOW MOVEMENT CAN ENHANCE YOUR VIDEO

There are different ways how adding action can make your video more interesting to watch:

- Action can grab attention at the start of the video.

- Movement can bring your subject to life.

- Action can direct the viewer's attention to specific elements.

- Movement keeps your viewers engaged. It's more interesting to watch something move than to look at still images.

- It can help you visually demonstrate what you're talking about.

- Movement can convey an atmosphere or feeling.
- In people, movement can reveal character and personality.

> Whether you're capturing a new office building, making a product video, or creating an instructional video of a new interface, movement can draw your viewers into your story and bring your subject to life.

Filming a building? Make sure to capture some form of movement; wait for someone to enter the building or a car to pass by. Filming a fruit bowl? Slide the bowl into the frame, or take an apple out of the bowl. So, for every shot, think: how can I add action to this scene?

It's about thinking differently, not just looking at what you see now but also at what could potentially happen.

Filming a boring, empty hallway with no movement? Ask a colleague to walk (or jump/bike/dance) through the hallway, throw something into the frame, or open a door.

TWO SIMPLE WAYS TO ADD MOVEMENT TO ANY SHOT:

1. Move the camera.

2. Move what's in front of the camera.

Adding movement to your shots doesn't have to be complicated. You might just have to learn to film things differently. And that is as simple as moving the camera or what's in front of it.

Moving the camera itself usually isn't hard—many people naturally follow the action or instinctively move toward a subject. The real challenge often lies in creating action shots when not much is happening on its own.

> Time to film again! Grab an object, anything close to you right now. You're going to make shots with action, but there's one rule: you can't move the camera.
>
> Instead, focus on creating movement in front of your camera lens. What can enter or exit the frame? Can you move or shift something? How can you show objects in action? Can you try filming in timelapse (speeded up) or slow motion (slowed down)? Try it out. How does this highlight the movement in your shots?

Say you're filming a pretty boring work-situation: a group of colleagues meeting in an unimaginative colorless room. Instead of settling for one predictable eye-level shot, capture movements in multiple shots filmed from different perspectives:

- A wide view of coworkers entering the room, filmed in timelapse (sped up)
- A low-angle shot filmed from the table of a colleague opening a laptop
- A close-up of someone grabbing a pen
- A time-lapse of a colleague drawing on a board
- A medium shot of a door opening, showing the meeting in action
- A close-up shot of two colleagues talking to each other
- An eagle-eye view of a colleague taking notes

Filming movement: close-up of someone grabbing a pen

Notice something is happening in all these shots. There's action (even if it's just slight movement). Did you also notice that all these shots have different angles? It's a variety of distance and angle that makes a video interesting to watch.

You know how this will help you? With just these six shots, you'll be able to edit a visual story in no time.

Good filming techniques can help speed up the edit process. If you capture a variety of shots, stitching them together to craft a story becomes easy.

It's time to put theory into practice! Walk over to a water faucet. Grab your phone and make two shots in slow motion.

- Open your camera app and look for the slow-motion feature (this varies by phone; on most devices, you can find this option by swiping left in the recording menu or looking for "pro camera tools").

- For shot one, turn on the water tap and record for three seconds. For shot two, repeat the process, but this time, create some action by splashing the water, for example, by moving your hand through it.

- Now, watch both recordings. Do you see the difference? When the motion is predictable (as in shot one), slow motion doesn't have a big impact. But when there's action (like splashing water), it becomes much more interesting to watch!

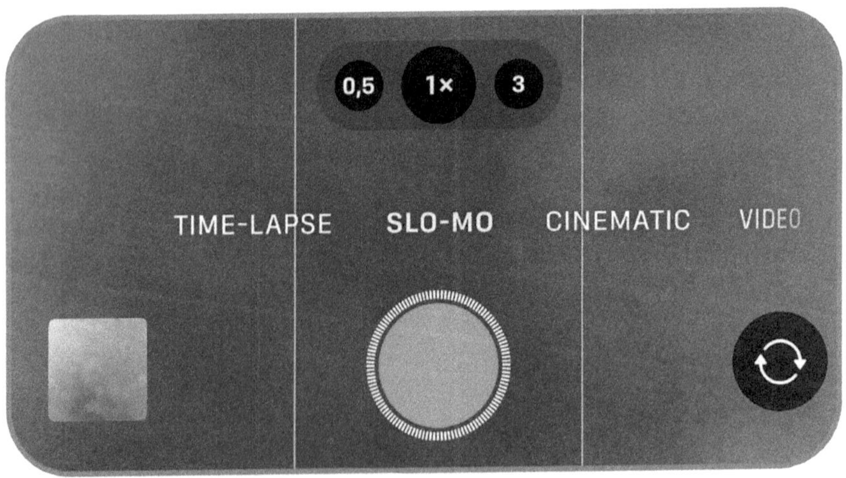

Timelapse speeds up the video, while slowmotion slows down the action

Now that you've seen what movement can do for the dynamics of your shots, let's take it a step further. For the previous exercises, you've kept the camera still; it's time to practice moving your camera.

ACTION-PACKED FILMING: HOW TO SPICE UP YOUR VIDEOS WITH ACTION SHOTS

How do you move your camera in a way that suits the shot, your video, and your viewer? A quick whip pan (fast camera movement) at the start of a video can capture attention and make someone stop scrolling. Adding a fun transition between shots introduces an element of surprise, tempting people to keep watching. But how do you apply this in your own branding videos?

It's amazing to see that the principles I learned in traditional film classes at the University of North Texas, with big traditional studio cameras, seamlessly transfer to filming with a phone. Back then, I used large dollies and camera sliders. Now, I apply the same techniques but with small gimbals, selfie sticks, and even napkins. The tools have changed, but the filmmaking techniques stay the same.

Five practical ways to move your smartphone camera for captivating recordings:

ADD MOVEMENT BY ZOOMING IN/OUT:

One movement you're probably familiar with: zooming in or out. Never digitally zoom while filming because you may lose some of your image quality. If you want to capture a subject up close, don't zoom on your screen, but move your phone closer to the object or person. The more you zoom, the lower the quality. For example, if you want to show the details of a product, bring your phone closer to the product for a close-up shot. If zooming while filming gets a bit shaky, consider applying a digital zoom in post-production. During editing, you have control over the speed and amount of zoom, giving you a smoother and more polished result.

PANNING: ACTION FROM LEFT TO RIGHT

"Panning" is a term often used in videography. You typically use a pan to give a wide impression of a place or to follow a subject. Hold your smartphone in a fixed position and rotate the camera from left to right or vice versa. The key is that the phone doesn't move from its spot, so you, the videographer, stay in the same place. For instance,

Using the books as foreground, I'm panning (filming from left to right)

create a shot of your workplace or an event with your wide-angle lens: move your phone slowly from left to right. This gives viewers a complete view of the environment.

TRACKING SHOTS WHERE YOU MOVE ALONG

In a tracking shot, you move the camera horizontally from left to right or the opposite, just like panning. But in a tracking shot, the camera doesn't stay at a fixed point. You move along with the subject. This keeps the subject continuously in view while the background changes. This can be very useful for action shots.

On many modern phones, you can turn on an action mode, keeping the subject in focus while you move along. You can, for example, follow a colleague getting a cup of coffee or walk along with a machine on the factory floor.

TILT YOUR PHONE FOR GRAND SHOTS

Want to make that nice building or beautiful hall look even grander? Tilt your smartphone up or down while filming, and for an even grander effect, use your wide-angle lens. For example,

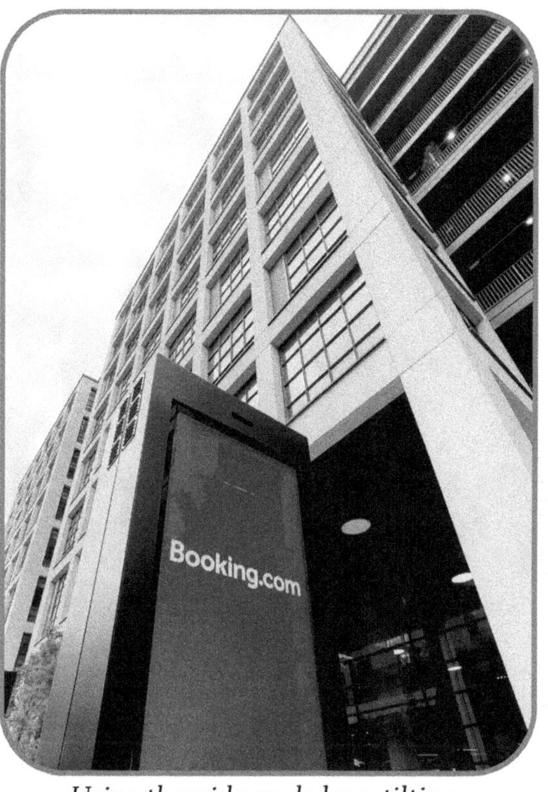

Using the wide angle lens, tilting the camera up for a grand effect

stand at the bottom of a building with your phone close to the ground, and tilt your phone up. This is also the perfect movement to show complete outfits during fashion shoots; tilt your phone from top to bottom or vice versa to showcase the whole outfit. Is it about a unique floor design? Tilt your phone from top to bottom for a grand effect.

CREATE A SLIDER SHOT IN SLOW MOTION

One of the best ways to make your videos look more professional is through a slide shot. You can use slider tools for this, but it's not necessary. Place your phone on a stable surface,

such as a table, floor, cabinets, or window sills. Turn the phone so the lens films close to the surface, and smoothly slide your phone from left to right or the opposite. It's helpful to place a napkin or a small towel under your phone to stabilize the shot.

Creating a slider shot with the camera lens low, while the phone slides on a towel

Want to make the shot even more impressive? Set your phone to slow-motion mode. Done well, you get shots that look very professional but are simply filmed with your phone and a napkin.

PLAY WITH DEPTH OF FIELD

Another technique that makes your videos look like they were shot by a professional: playing with depth of field. Your smartphone automatically focuses each shot. But you can also tell your phone where you want it to focus. Simply tap a different spot on your screen to change the focus. For example, if you bring a product close to the camera (3–5 cm from the lens), you can first focus on the background, making the product blurry. Then tap on the product, making the product sharp and the background blurry. A change in depth of field can give your viewer focus in the story and often looks very professional immediately.

Regular video (left) versus cinematic mode (right)

Time for a new filming exercise! You're going to create a few shots of this book, testing out the techniques we talked about:

- Slide shot: place the book on a table. Put your phone on the book (camera low) and slide across the cover to reveal the title.

- Tilt your phone to capture the title on the spine; try filming this with different lenses to see how each shot differs.

- Put your phone in slow-motion mode, film in eagle-eye perspective, and flip through the book.

- Low slide shot: Place your phone on the table with the camera low, then slide it from left to right, bringing the book's cover into view.

- Practice with depth of field: put the book on a table, put your lens up close, and play with focus to highlight different parts of the book.

FILM LIKE A PRO WITH CINEMATIC OR PORTRAIT MODE

Imagine taking a video with your smartphone, and later, you get to choose which part you want to in focus and which part you want to be a bit blurry. That's what filming in cinematic mode can do!

> Cinematic mode lets you decide where the camera should focus even after you've already taken the video.

So, how does it work? Cinematic or portrait film mode on smartphones often works by using multiple lenses to capture a scene from slightly different perspectives. The phone's software analyzes this information to understand the distance of objects in the video. It creates a depth map, which what lets you later adjust the focus, even after the video has been recorded. You decide what you want to keep sharp and what parts of the video you want to make blurry.

Not all smartphones support a cinematic mode, digital rack focus or similar cinematic features. But, smartphone technologies change very fast, and new models with enhanced features are released all the time. So, for the most up-to-date information on these types of functionalities, check the official websites or reviews of the latest smartphone models from major manufacturers.

GRAB YOUR VIEWERS' ATTENTION WITH TEXT & GRAPHICS

Text in your video is more important than ever. And, it's more accessible than ever too, thanks to user-friendly edit-tools on platforms like TikTok, Instagram, and YouTube.

A few reasons why adding text or graphics to your videos can help grab and keep attention from your viewers:

- On-screen text makes sure that the most important information stands out. Your audience not only hears and sees the message but also reads the message.

- Text promotes inclusivity, making your content accessible to a broader audience, including those who prefer reading or have hearing impairments.

- Strategically placed text can encourage your viewers to take action, whether it's subscribing, visiting a website, or engaging with your content.

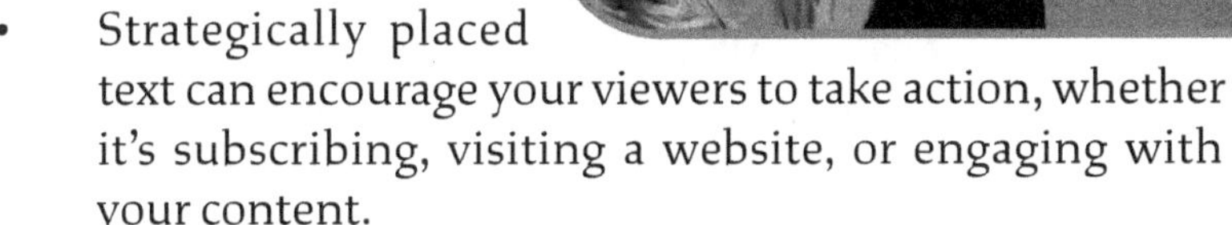

When and where you place your text will change the way you film. Make sure there's enough room for your main message by framing your shots thoughtfully. Leave some space above someone's head or below a product; that way, there's some room for text in the editing phase. And don't forget about captions or subtitles; you have to keep in mind the safe margins on different platforms.

Some practical tips for text placement in your videos:

- Frame It Right: Frame your shots with an eye on where text might go. Leave room above a head or below a product, keeping in mind where text could be added later.

- Top Spot for Headlines: Stick the essential text, like headlines or key messages, at the top of your video. Just be mindful about those safe margins for the platform you're posting on.

- Caption Savvy: If you're using captions, throw them in the lower part of the screen—not too low, though. Those safe margins are often higher than you'd think! On Instagram, for example, it's best to skip the lower quarter to dodge overlap with platform buttons.

- Timing's Everything: Make sure your text pops up at the right moments. Sync it with your narrative—if you're talking about an interesting statistic, show the number right when you talk about it.

Text doesn't just make your message more visible and memorable; every time a word or graphic appears, it triggers your viewer to keep watching. And isn't that what we want?

MAKE YOUR VIDEOS SPARK WITH EYE-CATCHING TRANSITIONS

If you spend time on Instagram or TikTok, you've likely come across video transitions. A very common one is placing your hand on the lens after one shot and then removing it for the next. If you'd add a similar transition digitally in the edit, it's known as a "fade to black" (after all, there is a slight moment the screen is black). But, you can also create these transitions during filming.

Filming transitions can be a fun and fresh way to guide your audience seamlessly from one shot to the next. You can place things on the camera lens or move the camera itself. It's often not very complicated, but planning your shots in advance is key.

I've created many videos of my speaking gigs at various venues. Often, the shots are similar: arriving, capturing the audience, and shots of me speaking. They're a bit boring and predictable. Here's how I used a transition in one of my videos to spice things up a bit.

- Shot 1: I filmed myself outdoors in front of a venue, and without stopping the camera, I placed the phone (camera) on the ground, and simulated stepping on the lens.

- Shot 2: I uncovered the lens (with my foot) on the floor of a grand stage and then put the camera into the air while standing onstage, capturing the audience turning around.

In just six seconds, I introduced a different environment and ambiance, adding a fun surprise to the video! This is why I love filming transitions. They can help you infuse surprises into your video that otherwise might have been a bit boring and predictable!

Shot one: outside and 'stepping' on the lens. Shot two: on stage

If you think transitions are fun but not for your business, think again. I've literally helped hundreds of companies make their videos spark a bit more using transitions. For practically all topics, professions, and industries, you can incorporate transitions into your videos. It's often not about the subject but how you film it, and especially whether you can think outside the box when you're creating your video plan.

1. **Hair Salon/Fashion Stylist - Transformation:**

    Shot 1: Display the person facing the camera with the current hairstyle and then have them turn their back toward the camera.

    Shot 2: Begin with the person facing away, then spin around to reveal the new haircut.

2. **Real Estate - Blueprint to Furnished:**

   Shot 1: Exhibit a blueprint, design, or bare bones living room. Then, quickly pan the camera to the right.

   Shot 2: Pan the camera to the right and reveal a beautiful fully furnished property.

3. **Educational Institution - Classroom Engagement:**

   Shot 1: Present a quiet and empty classroom. Film yourself standing in the middle of the room, and clap.

   Shot 2: Film yourself in the middle of the same room, and clap. This time, there are students around you in an engaging/interactive session.

4. **Restaurant - Busy Dining Evolution**

   Shot 1: Capture an empty dining area. Quickly lift the camera up to the ceiling.

   Shot 2: Start with pointing your camera toward the ceiling and quickly tilt down, revealing a lively, bustling crowd.

5. **Travel/Tourism: Trip Surprise**

   Shot 1: Film someone in their home, walking out with suitcases, closing the door.

   Shot 2: Film that same person opening a door (similar distance as the previous shot) on a completely different location with a beautiful view.

6. **Communication - Meeting Dynamics**

   Shot 1: Depict a virtual meeting setup. Then quickly pan the camera left.

   Shot 2: Pan the camera left to reveal an in-person meeting, showcasing a team collaboration.

7. **Vehicle Business - Reveal**

    Shot 1: Zoom in by moving the camera closer to a specific car part or a logo.

    Shot 2: Zoom out to unveil the entire, fully-assembled vehicle.

8. **Any job - Workspace Transition**

    Shot 1: Show a cluttered desk. Then move your hand over the camera lens.

    Shot 2: Move from a hand covering the camera to uncovering, unveiling an organized workspace.

9. **Designers/Engineers - Blueprint to Reality**

    Shot 1: Display a blueprint or design. Insert a pen that taps the design.

    Shot 2: Remove the pen in frame (tapping at the same distance), and reveal the constructed project or product.

10. **Electricians - Lighting Transformation:**

    Shot 1: Start in a room that's badly lit. Place your hand in front of the lens and snap your fingers.

    Shot 2: Move your snapping fingers (at the same distance as shot 1) and reveal a well-lit space after fixing lights.

11. **Event Planning - Vibrant Transformation:**

    Shot 1: Present an empty event venue. Then, quickly tilt the camera down.

    Shot 2: Tilt the camera up and showcase a lively atmosphere with attendees at a vibrant and bustling event.

12. **Fitness Trainer - Exercise:**

Shot 1: Film a person doing a basic exercise. Have them put their hand or foot over the camera lens.

Shot 2: Let the same person uncover the camera lens and show them performing an advanced exercise, emphasizing the right way to do an exercise.

13. **Dentist Office - Before and After Smile:**

Shot 1: Showcase a patient's smile before a dental procedure. Then whip the camera up quickly.

Shot 2: Whip the camera down quickly and reveal the transformed and improved smile after the dental work.

14. **Florist - Bouquet Reveal:**

Shot 1: Lay a bunch of "random" flowers on a table. Then, put a vase in the frame and tap it.

Shot 2: Tap the vase (same distance, same spot) that now holds a vibrant bouquet of the flowers that were just on the table.

15. **Any job - Cheers to Working Here:**

Shot 1: Show to coworkers in their workspace, and then move the camera close to them doing a toast/cheers. They could be toasting with coffee, markers, designs, or simply doing a high-five.

Shot 2: Start with a close-up of a toast/high-five of the same coworkers, then zoom out, and they're in a different location—perhaps they've finished that awesome project, are on an amazing work trip, or at a fun event.

You don't need to add a transition in every video. In fact, you don't want to because a transition often requires more planning and filming time. So, please keep in mind: use a transition only if it truly adds something to the video.

> Now it's your turn! Time for a filming exercise. All you need is your phone and this book you're reading.
>
> Shot 1: Place your phone inside the book and hit record. Now slowly close the pages. Voila! You've just created a classic "fade to black."
>
> Shot 2: Switch your phone to selfie mode and hit record. Hold your lens against the cover of the book (so you get a black screen), and quickly move the phone back to reveal the book. You can also make a selfie shot, so the viewer sees not just the book, but you too!
>
> The final step is to blend these two shots. If you have some editing experience, join the shots exactly where the screen goes black at the end of shot 1 and starts black at the beginning of shot 2.
>
> No editing experience? No worries. Later in this book, you'll get to know a few great apps you can use to edit your videos.
>
> YES! You've just made your own transition. I'd love to see the result, so share it with me on your socials!

You've now done various exercises around capturing movement, and you've discovered how filming from different perspectives can make your video a lot more interesting.

You can now make engaging shots from situations that might initially look boring simply by filming with movement and from various angles and distances.

You've practiced action shots, filmed objects, played with transitions, and now you're going to do something most people find even scarier: filming people.

5
FILMING PEOPLE: YOUR GUIDE TO MAKING THEM SHINE

What's the main reason you stop scrolling and keep watching a video?

You now know that action and cool camera tricks can help grab attention and add visual surprises. But that's often not the biggest reason to keep watching.

The main reason you stay tuned into a video is the person in it. After years of making videos and analyzing stats, one of the biggest things I always apply in businesses is to center the video around people.

Does the person have to look perfect and speak the words perfectly? No. The most important thing is whether they come across as trustworthy. So, the biggest question isn't who's the most attractive but who does your viewer want to see?

Think about it. Why do you keep watching a video? It's not just the beautiful camera tricks or flashy editing. Most of the time, it's the person in the video. Do you trust them? Do you feel at home with them? Do you believe what they're saying? If the answer is yes, you're much more likely to keep watching the video. If you don't feel that connection, then you're more likely to scroll on.

In this chapter, you'll learn how to film people. You'll start with the techniques. Where should you place the camera? How close or far should you be? But more importantly, how do you capture a person truly as a human? How can you make someone feel relaxed and authentic in front of your camera?

HOW TO FILM SOMEONE: YOUR TECHNICAL GUIDE

If you want the focus on the person on screen, you have to avoiding filming techniques that can distract viewers. For example, positioning the camera too low can unintentionally give the impression that you're looking down on your audience. And if you forget to check the background, it can lead to awkward visuals like a lamp post seemingly sprouting from someone's head. So, let's start with a few technical checks!

SET THE CAMERA AT EYE LEVEL

Every day, you make contact with people by looking into their eyes, preferably at about the same level. The same goes for the placement of the camera. If you place the camera too low, you're looking down on the viewer. It's a simple technique often used in films; place the camera low to make someone look powerful, large, or arrogant. If you place the camera high, the viewer looks down on you. This technique is used to make someone appear smaller, powerless, or childlike. And that's probably not what you're aiming for with your video. So, place the camera lens roughly at the same height as the eyes of the person in front of the camera.

*Filming with
the camera high*

*Filming with
the camera low*

Nowadays, people love to film from a high angle (goodbye double chin, hello beautiful light!). But for business videos with a professional goal, I recommend placing the camera at eye level. When you meet someone in person, you prefer to talk at eye level; it's the most natural way to have a conversation.

Let's do a short exercise again. Grab your phone, open your camera app, and switch it to selfie mode. Now film three shots of yourself. First, hold the camera lens low. For the second shot, hold it high. And finally—your third shot—try to film at eye level. Now, look back at the shots you made. What does the height of the lens do? How do you perceive yourself in each shot?

HOW FAR AWAY SHOULD YOU BE FROM THE LENS?

Open you camera app on your phone, and look at the screen. This is your video canvas, your creative playing field! You decide where to put people in the frame—left, middle, right, close up, far away.

> There are standard framing and composition techniques, but framing is subjective. What one person loves, another person might find awful. So, try out some composition techniques you find in this book, but also play around with what you personally like!

Here are a few standard techniques and composition rules for filming a person.

CLOSE-UP

In a standard close-up, you leave a bit of space above the head with the shoulders in view. Why choose a close-up? Close-ups can create a sense of closeness, can make the viewer feel like they're getting to know you, and they're effective at building trust. Plus, if your viewers watch your videos on phones, close-up shots can be very effective as well. If you stand closer to the camera, you appear larger in compact screens.

MEDIUM SHOT

If you want to show a little bit of the surroundings, a medium shot is perfect. A standard medium shot is from about the chest to right above the head. A medium shot and medium-long shots can be used for a reporter or interviewer walking around at an event because the viewer can see the environment as well as the reporter. The medium shot and the medium-long shots are also often used for interviews.

LONG SHOT

A long shot, also known as a "full body shot," shows the whole body from head to toe. It's a wide shot, usually used to show the environment. It's a perfect way to give viewers a feel of the location but less suitable to make a personal connection with them. That's why it's wise to use a combination of long shots and medium/close-up shots.

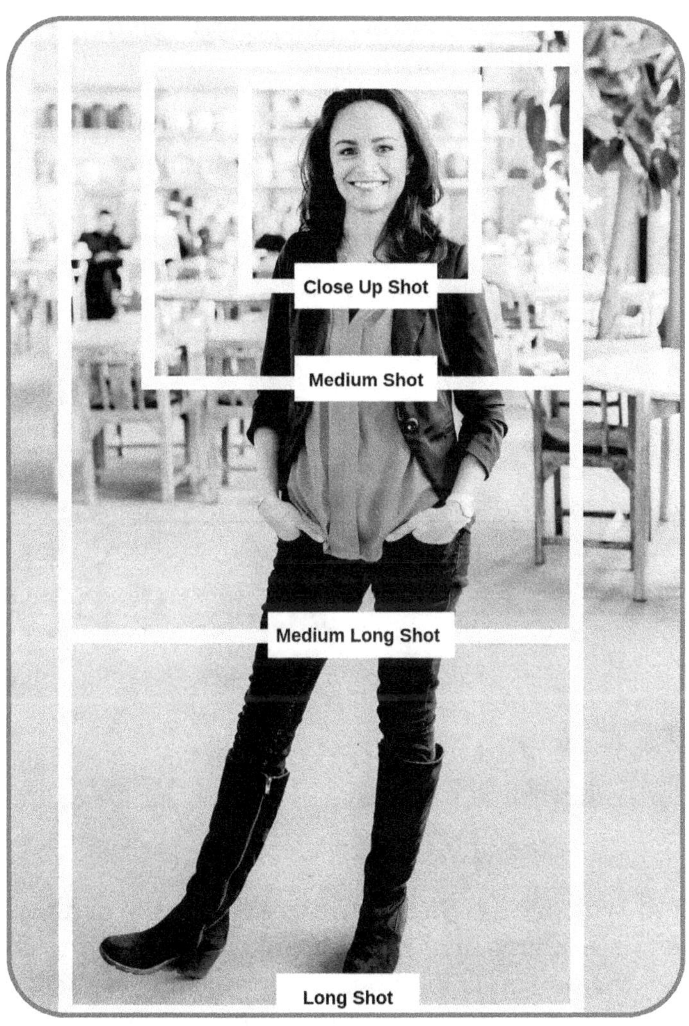

Common types of framing shots

RULE OF THIRDS

If you open up the camera app on your phone, do you see a white grid—four thin lines on your screen? The white lines divide the image into nine equal sections. It's used to apply the rule of thirds, a widely used composition rule to help you decide where to place your subject in the frame.

Research shows that a shot is more interesting when the subject is on one of these lines or intersections. This might sound complicated, but it's not.

So, to put it simply, you don't place the person in the middle of the frame but a bit to the right or left side on one of the lines. When you use this technique, you create space in your image, so the viewer's attention goes to the person.

Use the rule of thirds while filming a person

How do you decide whether to place the person on the right or left in the frame? The main rule of thumb here is to check where the person is looking, and make sure the person is always turned toward the open space in the canvas. So, if the person is on the right side of the grid (looking to the left), make sure there's space on the left side of the frame. More often than not, the side that feels just right is the correct one!

> Ready to try it out? Turn on the grid on your phone and let's apply these techniques. Activating the white grid lines on your phone is not difficult. For iPhones, head to your phone's settings, tap on the camera, and then go to "Grid" or "Guidelines." Android phone? Open the camera app, enter the settings, and enable the grid option.

DON'T FORGET TO DO A BACKGROUND CHECK

Once you've got the person at eye level and nailed down the ideal framing distance, it's time for a quick background check. The focus of the viewers should be on the message and the person. So, ask yourself: does the background enhance the message, or is the background a bit distracting?

It can be quite disappointing to wrap up a shoot, all set for editing, only to discover an awkwardly placed tree "growing" out of someone's head in the background. Editing that out afterward can be a real challenge. Sure, there are AI tools that can remove specific elements from your video, but it's far quicker and simpler to nail it in the filming stage.

> You want the attention to be on the message, on the person. So, does the background add to the message, or does it distract?

MAKE EYE CONTACT - LOOK INTO THE LENS

Do you know where the camera lens is on your phone? You might be able to point it out now, but when you're filming in selfie mode, do you look at the camera lens or at yourself on the screen?

When filming in selfie mode, a lot of people end up looking at themselves—not the camera lens. And by looking past the lens, they're missing direct eye contact with the viewer. Whether it's a vlog, a how-to video, a goofy dance, or a serious interview, you want to connect by looking into the camera lens because that's how you make that direct eye contact with your audience.

So, why film in selfie mode instead of turning your phone around to use the back camera? I know creators who swear by the latter. If you use the back camera, you avoid the constant distraction of seeing yourself, and often, the back camera shoots in higher quality.

 My personal preference is using selfie mode when I film myself. Why? Because it allows me to see myself, the background, and keep track of how long I've been filming. It's what works for me.

As I mentioned earlier, it can be distracting to constantly face your own reflection, especially if you're a bit camera-shy. So, do what rocks your boat, what makes your cookie crumble—whatever brings you the most joy in front of the camera! Try it out and see what works best for you..

HOW A POST-IT NOTE CAN HELP WITH FOCUS

If you find yourself feeling too distracted in selfie mode, constantly looking at your own reflection, here's a handy trick: block the view of your own face. Yep, block your face!

Grab a Post-it Note, a small cloth, or a piece of paper, and place it over the screen. Make sure to do this after checking the lighting and framing, of course, right before hitting the record button.

It's a super simple little trick that can shift your focus from yourself to the viewer and your story. Many of my course participants say that this simple adjustment truly helped them speak better in front of a camera. So, why not give it a shot?

Do you keep looking at yourself while filming? Put a
Post-it Note over your screen so you can focus on the lens!

HOW TO ENSURE SOMEONE LOOKS IN THE CAMERA LENS

If you're interviewing someone, and you want them to look directly into the camera lens, make sure to explain this beforehand. Don't just point to the camera, but also clarify who they're talking to: the viewers.

> It's crucial that the person in front of the camera knows who they are talking to. You probably have a clear understanding of the target audience, but the person in front of the camera might not.

If you stand next to your phone during the interview, you might notice that the person still looks at you instead of the camera. And that makes sense because it's much more natural to talk to a person instead of a camera. To avoid this, try standing directly behind the phone. Hide your head behind your phone so that the person you're interviewing looks straight into the camera lens.

If the person in front of the camera still tries to make eye contact with you, you can try taking a few large steps to the left or right, so you are completely out of sight. It's a simple method to "force" them to look into the camera lens instead of you. Try and see what works for you.

HOW TO BE IN FRONT OF THE CAMERA TOGETHER

Are you sitting next to the person you're interviewing? Or are you perhaps doing a quick vlog with two or three people in front of a camera? Don't forget to look into the camera lens!

If you're having a conversation, it's much more natural to look at the person(s) you're talking to. But if you don't look into the camera lens, you're not involving the viewer in your conversation. So, make sure to always start and end the video looking at the camera, and try to involve the camera (the viewer!) in your conversation.

> Pretend the camera is another person joining the conversation, but not just another person—the most important person at the table.

You do this by nodding, smiling, and talking to the camera lens. It might feel a bit unnatural to do at first, but keep practicing. Remember that you want the viewers to feel like you are talking to them; you want them to feel like they are a part of the conversation.

THREE WAYS TO FILM AN INTERVIEW

Think about the composition of interview shots before you go out on the interview: how far the camera will be from the person if he/she is going to look into the camera or past the camera to the interviewer. Here are some of the most-used interview composition shots.

1. LOOKING PAST THE CAMERA

The person you're interviewing is looking past the camera to the interviewer. This usually results in a pretty natural conversation because the person who is being interviewed can talk to another human being, the interviewer. It's great for people who are not used to talking to a camera. When you're filming by yourself, it might be helpful to use the front camera of your phone (selfie camera) so you keep an eye on the composition, lighting, and video duration while you're filming.

Person being interviewed looking past the camera

2. LOOKING AT THE CAMERA

The person you're interviewing is looking in the camera lens. This composition shot is perfect to connect with the viewer and make a video feel more personal because of the direct eye contact. At the same time, talking to a camera can feel a bit unnatural. So, if the person who is being interviewed is nervous or not used to talking to a camera, this can be a bit tricky.

> Remember, you're never just talking to a camera. You are talking to a person.

My sister Joseffa, her husband David, and my son Liam
filming together YouTube.com/JoseffaTrip

3. SEVERAL PEOPLE IN FRONT OF THE CAMERA

People tend to get nervous or stiff in front of a camera. One way to make people loosen up is by having several people in front of the camera together.

> One of the scariest things to do? Be on camera. One of the best ways to take away nerves? Be on camera together.

Talking with two or three people is a lot different than talking alone. If you're interviewing coworkers, for example, and they're stumbling through their nerves, try to put two people in front of the camera at the same time. You often see the dynamics change in an instant.

Keep in mind that putting several people in front of a camera is not always the right solution. Every person who's visible on the screen needs to be there for a reason; there shouldn't be just one person talking while the other one stays silent. If it's a back-and-forth conversation where both people are speaking, being together on camera can be a much more fitting and natural way to capture the dialogue.

I've conducted many on-camera interviews, and in most of them, I'm not visible. You only see the person I'm interviewing because they carry the narrative. The only reason for me to appear on camera is if I'm contributing to the conversation. If you don't see me talking, there's no point in me being in the shot.

If you're considering putting two or more people in front of the camera, think about this: Is it necessary for everyone to be visible? Does each person add something to the conversation?

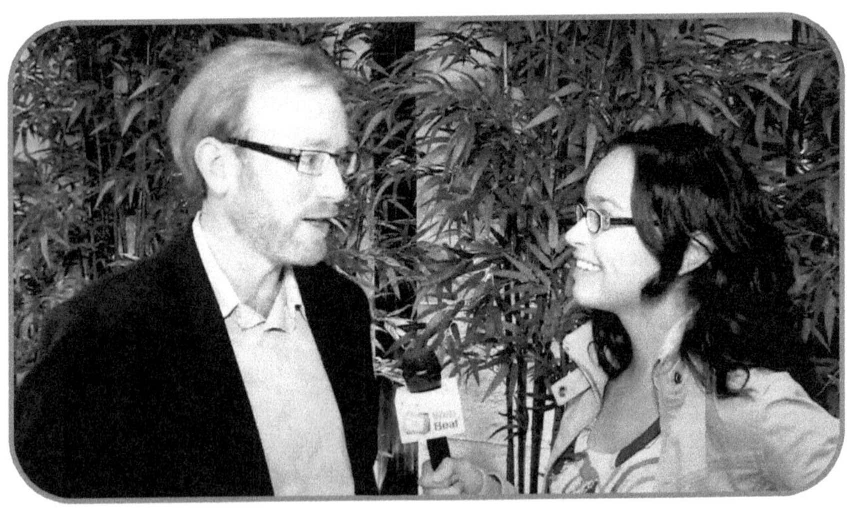

Interviewing Richard MacManus, founder of ReadWriteWeb at SXSW. We're both on screen because we both add to the conversation

4. OVER THE SHOULDER

This is exactly what it sounds like: The camera points over the shoulder of the interviewer. This way of interviewing is a bit more formal, reporter style. Since you can't keep a close eye on the camera when it's behind you, it might be handy to work with a camera operator for these types of inter-viewing shots.

The over-the-shoulder technique can be very useful if you're interviewing different people in a short amount of time, on the street or at events, for example. But keep in mind that not everyone will agree to a spontaneous interview, and make sure to bring video release forms so people can give official permission to use the footage.

Over-the-shoulder interview with Steve Harper, Entrepreneur, Author & Chief Rippler, at SXSW in Austin

HOW CAN YOU GET COMFORTABLE IN FRONT OF A CAMERA?

What if your doorbell rings right now, you open the door, and there's a camera crew standing there? If you were about to be interviewed, how would that make you feel? Are you getting nervous just reading these lines? Well, you're not alone. Most people are not exactly thrilled at the prospect of standing in front of a camera.

Sweaty palms, a pounding heart, and I could feel all my confidence slipping away. It was my first live TV news broadcast in 2008 at KDAF-TV in Dallas, Texas. I was standing in front of a huge touchscreen, ready to talk about a new app. I knew my script inside out. But when I faced the camera and the red light came on, I suddenly forgot how to use the touchscreen. I stumbled and stuttered through my rehearsed lines. My throat was tight with nerves, and my voice a good octave higher. It lasted only a minute but felt like forever.

When it was finally over, my boss stormed into the studio: "Where is Pelpina?"

I remember that so vividly because his question hit the nail on the head. Although I was physically present, I wasn't really there for the story or the viewer; my focus was consumed by my nerves.

Maybe you're naturally shy, or maybe you're insecure. It might be helpful to know that I am too. It took me years and lots of great people around me to have the courage to stand in front of the camera. And when I finally did stand in front of the camera, I was often so nervous that I stuttered, made up words (often to the great amusement of the news anchors), or froze and said nothing at all.

Every time you make a mistake, it's an opportunity to learn how to fix it. Every time you face your fears, you can learn how to overcome them. I now realize that every blooper, every nerve-wracking live segment, was part of my personal process.

> You don't learn much without making mistakes. And without facing your fears, you don't grow. So, keep making mistakes. Keep facing those fears. It's the only way to learn and grow!

A CAMERA IS UNNATURAL

Standing in front of a camera is quite strange. You're looking into a black circle, talking to it, laughing at it, and pretending it's a person. Pretty weird, right?

When you talk to a real person, you can look them in the eyes, and you usually get a smile back, and you can see if someone is listening to what you're saying. You can "read" the person and usually see if your message is coming across.

When you're in front of a camera, you get no feedback. You don't see how your viewer responds. So, how can you still come across as "real" and lively? How can you seem like a normal, talking person on camera?

> "Make a mess and clean it up later, and become a master at not caring what other people think."
>
> —Shay Rowbottom, CEO
> "Shay Rowbottom Marketing"
> and LinkedIn Video Influencer

DON'T FORCE YOURSELF TO DO EVERYTHING IN ONE TAKE

Say you make an educational video of about a minute and a half. Please don't try to record the whole minute-and-a-half story in one take. I did this a lot when I started out. The problem with this is if you mess up one time, you need to redo the whole story. Trust me, it can turn into a long and stressful video shoot.

Instead, divide your video into smaller parts, and record one part at a time. For example, you can divide an educational video into three tips. Record each tip separately. That way, you don't have to do your entire story perfectly in one take, and you can focus on one tip at a time. What's nice about this approach is that you can have a breather between each tip while you prepare yourself for the next tip!

> Don't try to record your video in one take. Instead, divide your video into smaller parts, and record one at a time.

AVOID WORD-FOR-WORD SCRIPTS

If you want to convey a message, then make sure you're not just "saying words" but striving to connect with the viewer.

You might have tried this before; you write a word-for-word script, hang it hanging next to the camera, and then try to read it off naturally. Most people fail terribly at this. Why? Because you write differently than how you speak.

> Quick exercise! Do you know how you speak? When I worked in TV news, it took me weeks to find my "speaking voice." That's because you write differently than you speak. And when writing scripts, it's useful to learn to write it in your speaking voice. Here's a quick exercise to discover how you naturally speak.
>
> - Switch your camera to selfie mode and hit record.
>
> - Tell a story for at least three minutes, maybe something special or nice that happened on a holiday or a funny incident you love to tell your friends about.
>
> - Watch your video back and write down exactly what you say. Note the exact words you speak.
>
> - What can you learn from this short clip? Do you speak in short or long sentences? Do you pause occasionally? Do you emphasize certain words? Do you use filler words?

Writing good word-for-word scripts isn't as easy as it seems, and reading these scripts naturally is even harder.

Now, you might be thinking, but if I don't write a script, how do I prepare? Not having a script isn't the same as being unprepared.

Always work with a focused video plan. Know your message, and know what you'll say, but don't rehearse the exact words you'll use. This way, you avoid sounding unnatural and monotonous. Usually, having a few keywords on paper and narrating from there works well. Compare it to giving a presentation at work. You wouldn't write it out and read it word for word to the group, would you?

HAVE TO USE A WORD-FOR-WORD SCRIPT? LET AI CORRECT YOUR EYE CONTACT

Sometimes, you can't avoid using a word-for-word script. If that's the case, remember to write as you speak. And if you notice that the person is not looking directly in the lens (because they're reading a script), you can even fix the eye contact issue with AI!

Take the Captions app, for example, which features an eye contact AI tool. It adjusts the direction of your gaze, making it seem as though you're looking into the camera lens. This way, you can peek at your keywords on a note next to the camera, and the app makes sure your eyes appear to stay on the lens.

> I tested the Eye Contact tool in the Captions app and am amazed at how well it works. It's as if the app has "stuck" eyes onto my face in the right color and size—and my eyes even continue to blink. But, if you zoom in and look closely, you can tell that my eyes have been digitally enhanced and occasionally drift slightly off. It's a tool in progress, but nonetheless, very impressive.

*The AI Eye Contact tool in the app
Captions corrects eye contact after filming*

Captions is just one app using this type of AI technology (and doing it remarkably well). But, of course, there are other apps embracing this technology, and undoubtedly many more tools and apps will start to incorporate this in the near future.

DON'T TALK TO A CAMERA, TALK TO A PERSON

Before you hit the record button, it helps to visualize exactly who you're talking to. Don't think of a broad target audience like "women aged thirty to forty-five," but imagine someone you personally know who fits into that category.

Picture your cousin Julia, your friend Rinke, or your neighbor Laura. Imagine that person in front of you and think: How would I tell her this story? If I ran into her on the street, how would I explain it? What words would I use, and how would I capture her attention?

> Just before you interview someone, point to the camera, and say: "This isn't just a camera. It's a person." Pin down who you're speaking to. The camera is just a tool for conveying a message; it's the eye of the viewer. Knowing who you're speaking to can help calm nerves and find the right tone and words for your audience.

HOW TO FILM WITHOUT FEELING HURRY OR PRESSURE

When you hit the record button, do you start speaking immediately? Do you feel the pressure to kick off right away? You might see the seconds ticking by on the screen, but actually, there's no need to rush. You can easily trim off the entire beginning of your video later.

> When you hit record, don't dive straight into talking. Allow yourself a moment to breathe. Give yourself some space to think.

One of the best ways to ease the pressure during filming? When you're about to record, don't start speaking immediately. Give yourself a moment to take a deep breath. Create some mental space to think: Who are you talking to? What do you want to convey? You can apply this when you're filming yourself but also when you're putting someone else on camera.

Don't hit record right before you start off with the first question. Instead, start recording well before the official conversation kicks off. This way, you allow the person in front of the camera to settle in and get comfortable before the big questions start.

> Want to calm someone down? Usually, saying, "Just relax," doesn't help. If someone is nervous, telling them, "You don't need to be nervous," often has the opposite effect.

Instead of pointing out what the other person could do differently, it often helps to lead by example. Say you want someone to be more relaxed on camera, then adopt a relaxed posture yourself. Want someone to speak softer? Lower your own voice.

Be mindful in interviews that your energy and demeanor greatly contribute to the atmosphere. Your goal is to create a comfortable environment that allows someone to be themselves on camera.

To minimize pressure during recordings, try the following for a more relaxed vibe:

- Avoid a rushed feeling, even if you are in a hurry. Instead, convey that there's plenty of time by saying, "We'll take all the time we need." This can take out the "rushed" feeling and often make the shoot a lot quicker.

- Do you have a perfectionist in front of the camera? Assure that you'll keep recording until they're satisfied, no matter how many takes it takes. This takes away the pressure to do it right in one take.

- Another tip for perfectionists: tell them they don't have to worry about how they speak. As the director, you're watching for the start of their sentences and the use of correct words. They can focus on telling their story. This takes away the pressure to speak with the right words.

- Do you notice they're afraid to make mistakes? Inform them that you can remove any mistakes during editing and ensure only their best takes are used.

People often make a recording out to be a bigger deal in their heads, and so they want it to go perfectly. Your job is to make it seem less daunting, and give people the freedom to make mistakes. When someone feels at ease in front of the camera, video recordings usually go much smoother.

People often ask about my camera routine. So, here it is!

When I record a vlog or educational video myself, I always follow a certain routine:

- I make a video plan and have a clear purpose for each clip I'll record.

- Before I press record, I think: Who am I talking to? What do I want them to know? I try to get into the right energy.

- When I press record, I take a few seconds. I breathe out to my belly, look into the camera (the person!), and start with a smile.

- If I make a mistake, I simply restart the sentence and keep going. I don't stop recording because of a slip-up. This way, I get a better flow. I can cut out the mistake(s) later.

- I try to remain calm until the very last second of the final sentence. Then I smile, breathe out, hold the last shot for two seconds, and stop recording.

Before I hit record, I pause, take a breath,
and imagine who I'm talking to

ONE MISTAKE AT A TIME

I don't know a lot of people who like to watch videos of themselves. It can be very difficult and just downright humiliating to see yourself stumble across a video segment. That's because you normally don't see yourself talking, and you're often hardest on yourself. You see everything that's wrong with you, from the way your voice sounds to the size of your forehead to how fast you blink.

Once you start making a lot of videos, it can be very helpful, though, to analyze yourself, hear your voice, and see your expression, how you hold your hands, and perhaps nervous habits. You first need to be aware of something before you can improve it, right?

When you watch your videos, you notice that you're not smiling, you're constantly hopping from one foot to the other, and your right hand keeps fiddling with your jacket. Instead of trying to tackle these three problems all at once, try to work on one at a time.

> Don't be too harsh on yourself; don't tackle too many problems at the same time. Focus on improving one skill at a time.

First, start off with working on your smile. For the next couple of videos, focus on smiling more. At first, it might feel fake or strange to force a smile. Keep practicing until the smiling becomes a new habit, part of your routine. But, give yourself some time to get used to it. You can learn a new habit in just one or two videos, but it could also take seven!

Once you've practiced this new habit and it's become a part of your routine, you move on to the next: standing still.

You don't want to tackle too many "problems" at the same time. If you focus on improving one skill, it becomes easier to handle. And eventually, it's all about learning new habits and making them a part of your routine.

> After booking our first skiing holiday (yes, at thirty-eight, I'd never been skiing), I enrolled in some classes. In the first lesson, I quickly realized there's a ton of things to learn all at once: how to avoid falling, proper foot placement, ski angles, maintaining an active posture . . . But the instructor constantly emphasized: focus on one thing at a time. So, at first, only concentrate on the placement of your feet. Once you've got that down, shift your attention to moving your weight from one foot to another. It's all about honing one skill at a time. The same principle applies to camera presence.

Learning to be comfortable, calm, and truly yourself in front of a camera—that's what it's about. And because that does not come naturally to most people, including me, give yourself some time and space to work on this. One skill at a time.

TIPS TO BECOME A STAR AT INTERVIEWING PEOPLE ON CAMERA

Interviewing people on camera can be quite the challenge, but when done right, a solid interview can be a fantastic foundation for your video.

So, how do you prepare for an interview? How do you make sure it doesn't turn into a rehearsed performance or feel like interrogation but becomes a natural conversation?

> A good interview doesn't feel like a prepared act, with pressure to use the right words. A good interview feels like a comfortable conversation where the words flow effortlessly.

Here are a few practical tips to make sure your interview feels like a natural conversation, from which you can extract valuable quotes for your video:

1. **<u>Prepare well.</u>**

   Before the interview, send or discuss a briefing with clear expectations, such as, "I am looking for one short quote of ten to fifteen seconds." Feel free to include a set of sample questions. These sample questions can serve as a great warm-up during the interview. I usually don't send the main questions beforehand, so I spontaneous and authentic responses to those questions.

2. **<u>Use a warm-up.</u>**

   Always assume that the person who is being interviewed needs to warm up a bit first. You can do this by asking a few simple "low-ball" questions. For example, ask about what they did that day and if they can introduce themselves or use the questions from the briefing. The length of the warm-up differs per person; that's something you'll have to sense during the interview. Once the person is warmed up, you can ask the main questions so that you get the natural answers.

Interviewing CEO All Your Bi Michael van Dijk, Rotterdam

3.   <u>**Start a normal conversation.**</u>

Try not to talk about the production and technical side of the interview. When you're setting up the camera and testing the audio, don't name everything that's happening. The person you're interviewing will only get more nervous when you say you're going to put the camera a little closer or if you count down before you hit record. Just try to have a natural conversation, which naturally flows into the actual interview.

4. **The best interviewers listen.**

Don't go through the list of questions one by one. Always listen to the person you're having a conversation with. The best interviewers don't ask questions; they listen. If you listen carefully, you can often come up with much more interesting questions than you had planned, the interview might go a lot deeper, and you will eventually come back with nicer quotes.

> If you get someone to laugh for a moment, even if it is just a small smile, it can help break the tension during a video shoot.

5. **Use humor.**

Don't be afraid to use humor, especially during business video shoots. For example, while setting up the lights, I might joke that it seems like the other person is at the dentist under those bright lights. I assure them that our interview will hopefully be a tad less painful than a dental appointment.

If you get someone to laugh for a moment, even if it is just a small smile, it allows the person to loosen up a little bit.

6. **<u>Stop and take a break.</u>**

Do you notice that it's not working? That the person you're interviewing is still super nervous and isn't able to get a word out of their mouth? Stop what you're doing.

Don't keep pushing. Take a quick break and do something completely different. Talk about a different subject, or let them take a quick walk around the block.

Something that also helps is to sit next to the person during that break. You step out of your role as interviewer/camera person and sit next to them as a person. A short break can often be very helpful; sometimes you only need a couple of minutes, but it can be exactly what you need for a much more relaxed interview!

7. **<u>Keep going!</u>**

I have trained hundreds of companies in making videos, and almost everyone makes the same mistake in the beginning: stopping the camera too often and too quickly.

Instead, just keep going!

> If someone misspeaks for a moment, do not stop the camera immediately to talk about the mistake. Keep recording and let the person start again with that specific sentence.

Stopping the camera repeatedly increases the chance that the person in front of the camera will get out of the "flow" of the story. This also applies to you. If you film yourself, and you make a mistake, resume the sentence and just keep going!

DO "SILLY" THINGS TO LOOK "NORMAL" ON CAMERA

Did you know that the most famous presenters and entertainers often still get nervous? The greatest singers often feel a massive bout of nerves before a show, no matter how often they perform. And people you see on TV daily might have developed "weird" routines to appear "normal" in front of a camera.

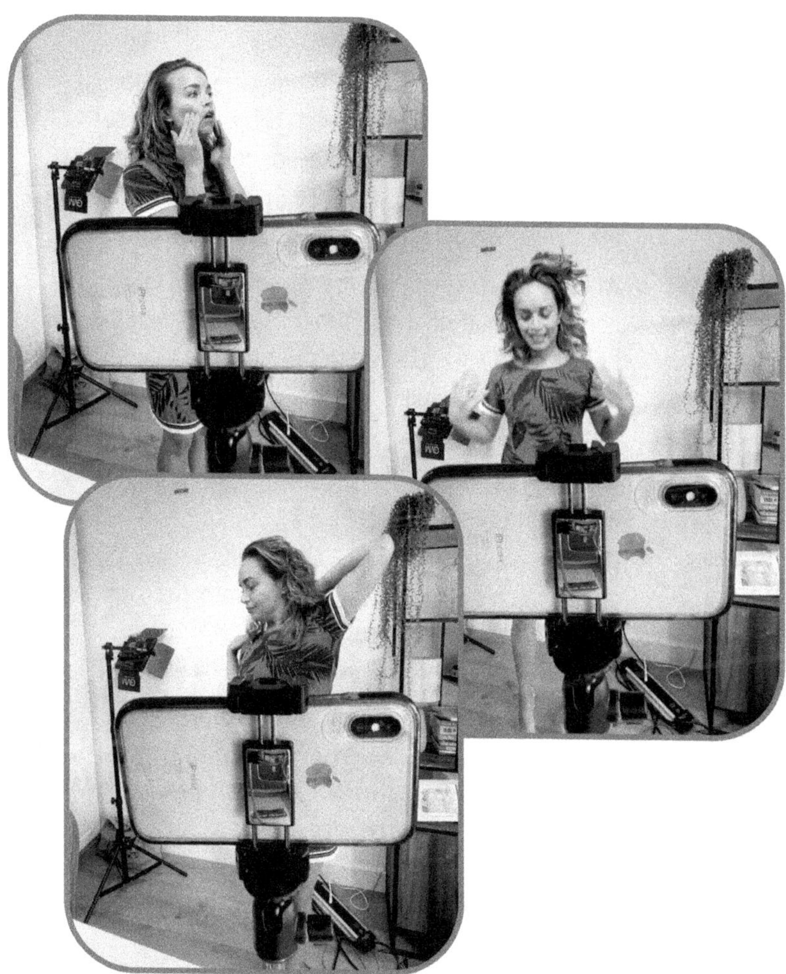

Stretching, jumping and voice/jaw exercises before I hit record

I sometimes lock myself in the bathroom to calm down right before a livestream. I often hardly eat before an important recording, and I still feel butterflies when I have to step onto a stage. After making literally thousands of videos and TV segments, people often think it all comes naturally to me and that I never get nervous anymore. Well, the opposite is true. How do I do this every day? My sister Joseffa is an actress, and we often say, "We do silly stuff to look normal on camera."

- When I'm nervous, I try to breathe slow and long. During my (many) voice liberation therapy sessions, I learned to exhale more, breathe lower (into the belly instead of the chest), and breathe slower. These exercises help bring me calmness and confidence.

- When I'm stressed, I force myself to let go by hanging upside down for a minute or two (with my head toward my knees). In this position, you literally have to let go. It calms me down, and helps me to regain focus.

- When I'm tired and don't feel like filming, I move my body. I pep myself up by playing music, singing, dancing, doing jumping jacks, or running for a few minutes. This eventually gets me into the right energy and gives me focus.

Yes, this list goes on, with more practical exercises I do to get into the right mindset. My sister Joseffa is an actress, and she also has some great insights about camera presence. We've compiled our experiences, stories, lessons, practical exercises, and tricks into our online course "Camera Confidence." Check out my website pelpina.com if you think this course could help you.

DON'T AIM TO GET CALM.
AIM TO BUILD YOUR TRUST.

What's the opposite of nerves and fear? Your answer might be calmness or peace. And that makes sense. When you get nervous, you often try to get calm—perhaps by adjusting your breathing or doing physical exercises. While these exercises can be hugely beneficial, what truly helps is shifting your mindset.

The opposite of fear isn't calmness. It's trust.

Take a moment to let that sink in. Instead of striving for calmness, focus on building trust. Trust the process. Trust your ability to deliver the message effectively. Have confidence and faith in your knowledge, and trust that you will articulate your words just right. In short, have a little more faith in yourself.

> Time for a quick exercise. You're going to create a confidence boost sheet. Start by writing down some compliments you've received that have stuck with you. What positive feedback has touched you? What do these compliments say about your presentation skills?
>
> Think about the people who give you confidence, who trust your ability. Imagine them standing behind you, lifting you, and carrying you. Write down their names.
>
> You can also write down quotes, poems, or sayings that always help you feel better about yourself. The goal of this sheet is to provide insight into yourself and, with just one glance, refill your confidence before a recording.

HOW DO YOU HANDLE NEGATIVE FEEDBACK ON YOUR VIDEOS?

Posting videos can sometimes feel like an open invitation for feedback. Everyone can and is allowed to have an opinion about your video (and thus about you), and that can feel quite vulnerable.

That's why having confidence in yourself is a beautiful foundation for your videos. If you have confidence in who you are, in your story and message, then it matters less what strangers think.

> Anyone can comment on your videos, but you decide what people you actually listen to.

American researcher Brene Brown has spent years studying shame and criticism. She says it's natural to fear criticism because you're neurobiologically wired to care about what other people think of you. But, you can choose which people are important to you. Frustrated strangers who leave a negative comment on your video? They're probably not that important to you. Leaving a nasty comment is easy. Making a video and daring to show a part of yourself? That's not so easy. It requires quite a bit of courage. Let only those who understand this give you sincere feedback.

A short exercise in dealing with negative feedback. When you receive a nasty comment, look at the sender. Who wrote this? Is this someone who whipped up a reaction out of emotion without deep knowledge or skill? Or is it someone who understands the subject, dares to make videos themselves, and gives you feedback that you can truly use?

Someone who has your best interest at heart might not always agree with what you do but will honestly tell you when you've messed up. They are also the ones who encourage you, who understand your goal, who help you to be vulnerable, and who cheer you on. This feedback often comes from a good place and helps you steer into the right direction.

So, is the critic standing beside you, wanting the best for you? Or are they, like the best helmsmen, standing ashore?

This feedback often comes out of emotion or frustration. The comment might come from someone with little knowledge on the topic, who often doesn't know you, and who doesn't understand your ultimate goal. This feedback often does not come from a good place and doesn't help you get in the right direction. If they're not standing beside you, then let that comment slide right off you.

6
VIDEO EDITING:
FAST & EASY
TIPS & TOOLS

This is the topic that generates the most questions in every lecture, training, or workshop I give. "What are the best editing apps?" And "How can you edit your videos faster?"

Do you want to make videos more efficiently? Start the editing process before you even begin editing. Sound strange? Well, it all boils down to good preparation, and that starts with a clear video plan. A good plan keeps you focused while filming. And if you film less, you often spend less time editing.

Before diving into cool editing tools and tricks to make editing more efficient (and more fun!), first take a close look at your video creation process. How can you make your entire content creation process quicker?

TIPS FOR TRIMMING BEFORE EDITING

Do you have a friend who seems to get things done super-fast? And you wonder how they manage it? The secret usually isn't all that exciting. Saving time often comes down to a tight routine, fewer choices, and clear rules.

Efficiency hasn't always been my strong suit. I love getting lost in the tiny details of a creative video edit. But after our first son was born, I had to find ways to do the same video editing work in less time. That's how I discovered methods to make editing a lot more efficient. And that, in turn, makes video editing a lot more fun!

If you smartly tackle planning and the filming process, you can save yourself a lot of time during editing. Here are three handy time-savers.

TIME TRIMMER 1. NEVER FILM JUST ONE VIDEO

So, you've got your equipment in place, you've set up excellent lighting, and you also have the right person in front of the camera . . . are you really only going to film just one video? Why not seize the opportunity to film several videos?

Say you're creating a video with a colleague sharing tips about a new installation. Instead of limiting yourself to one final video, why not transform each tip into a separate video? You could end up with a series of five videos from a single shoot, which gives you plenty of content for the coming weeks or months! This approach also applies to interviews—always maximize the content potential when you already have someone in front of the camera.

Richard Moore excels at repurposing video content. He ran a live one-hour Q&A every Monday for three years, simultaneously livestreaming to three platforms. He broke down the main recording into quotes, short videos, and mini articles, and effortlessly generated content for the entire week.

I always try to batch-shoot. Even for simple how-to videos on my social channels, I never settle for just one video, but at least three videos (And yes, I change shirts between takes to avoid questions about wearing the same outfit!) This way, a single video shoot gives me multiple pieces of content.

Richard Moore, founder of
Entrepreneur Business Live Events

TIME TRIMMER 2. FILM ONE-TAKERS

To save time, aim to get it right in one take. Sure, this seems straightforward and, yes, often easier said than done. So, how do you manage this?

1. **Take charge and steer toward usable quotes**

   Do you dare to interrupt someone during a recording? And then, do you have the courage to direct them toward usable quotes?

   Capturing one-takers might seem like a no-brainer, but it often fails because the person behind the camera finds it difficult to take control. So, if you're leading a recording and notice that a segment isn't going smoothly, take charge and direct until the piece is truly usable. It's often more efficient to repeat a tip or quote a few times during a recording so you don't have to edit it later. Repeating a segment until it's just right is usually quicker than editing mistakes afterward.

2. **Record in multiple layers simultaneously**

   You can also save a lot of time by recording in different layers at once. For example, you can make a screen recording while simultaneously doing a voice-over. You could first make a screen recording and then add the voice-over in an editing app, but if you can do it all at once, that's obviously faster.

Turn the microphone on during a screen recording to simultaneously record a voice-over

Another example is Apple's Clips app. With this app, you can make a recording that already includes graphics and live subtitles. This way, you can skip a step in the editing process, saving time.

> Time to try this out! Have you ever made a screen recording including a voice-over with your phone? It's really useful for tutorial videos. If not, give it a try now.
>
> On most iPhones, the screen recording button is in the control center (you need to have screen recording enabled in your settings). Hold the recording button for two seconds to turn your microphone on or off. On most Android phones, you can also start a screen recording from the quick settings panel.
>
> Don't have the function? There are various apps available for screen recording. My advice is to use an external microphone when recording a voice-over so your audio sounds professional. This way, you'll have your voice-over with visuals in one go!

TIME TRIMMER 3. WORK WITH A VIDEO FORMAT

Remember, piecing together an edit puzzle works best with a plan. Earlier in the book, you learned to divide your video into parts (intro, video bumper, quotes, outro) and estimate the time for each segment. Having a good plan will give you focus during filming and editing.

If you have a good video plan, you can reuse it. And that can then turn into a video format. A format can be a strategic blueprint for a video series. It's like having a mold or template that brings uniformity to all the videos in your series. Plus, having predefined formats can help make your entire video creation process more efficient.

Two video format examples I had a hand in crafting for the Dutch Red Cross:

Red Cross: Volunteers Stories

- Two-minute video
- Start with a powerful quote.
- Title, music, and short quotes tell the story
- B-roll to enhance
- End with the Red Cross logo and music

Red Cross: Street Talk

- One to two-minute video
- Short expert introduction
- Street interviews with short answers
- Expert provides deeper explanation
- End with the Red Cross logo and music

Having a predefined video format is like having a compass during the shoot—it guides your focus. Plus, it's a time-saver for editing because you can recycle graphics, intros, outros, and music.

START WITH ONE PILOT

If you decide to create a new video series, always start with a single pilot episode. This first episode is like your roadmap— it helps you nail down the vibe, from tone of voice to graphics and music. You get to see if everything flows the way you imagined.

So, take your time to make that pilot spot-on. It sets the stage for the whole series. This takes more time at the start, but it's worth the time investment. Once you've got that strong foundation, you're good to go for shooting and editing the entire series in one smooth ride!

HOW TO EDIT YOUR VIDEOS FASTER: 5 STEPS

Have you ever spent hours or days on a video edit, wondering if there was a quicker way? Editing is a creative process where you transform your shot clips into the envisioned story. But without the right approach, it can feel like you're trying to solve an endless puzzle.

I've edited thousands of videos and have definitely had my share of mishaps, especially in the early days. Man, I used to spend days editing! For years, I've worked with some big names in software: Avid, Adobe Premiere, and Final Cut Pro. And to be honest, for the really complex edits, my laptop is still my go-to.

But you know what really helped me save time on video editing? My phone. I now do most of my video edits with a few handy apps. Editing apps are often more straightforward and innovative than the professional editing software on my laptop. I work faster than ever, and I can edit anywhere I want.

This book isn't a step-by-step manual on editing in apps because the apps change quickly. If you're looking for comprehensive app tutorials, check out my online academy at pelpina.com. What will really save you a ton of time is developing a solid editing strategy. It's all about doing certain steps in the right order, no matter what editing app or software you use.

Follow these steps to save yourself a lot of time during the editing process:

1.   DELETE DURING THE VIDEO SHOOT.

Editing begins while you're filming. It can be frustrating to sift through sixteen identical-looking videos and wonder, "Which one was the right clip again?" So, during the video shoot, delete clips you know you won't use. If you've just recorded ten different clips, and was take number seven the best? Do yourself a favor and delete the other nine! Or, if you want to play it safe, simply tap the best clips as "favorite" or put them in a separate folder. This way, you keep the other clips as backups.

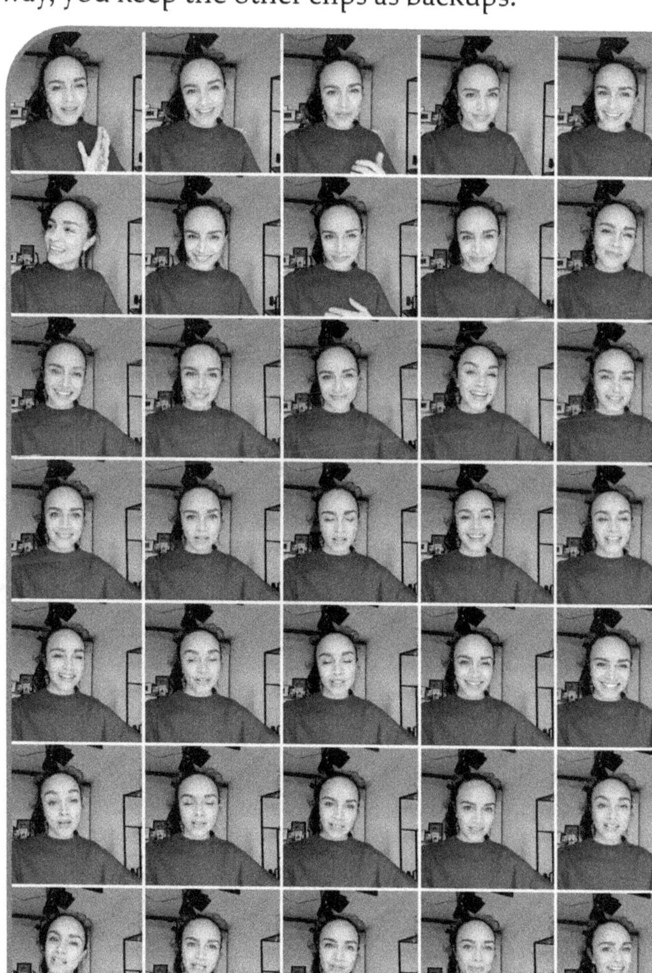

Avoid having too many similar videos in your camera roll. Delete during the shoot so you don't have to go through all the clips during the edit

2. PRESELECT THE RIGHT CLIPS & DO A ROUGH TRIM.

Go through all your footage and identify the best shots— the ones that must definitely be in the video. Make a pre-selection of these and put them in a separate folder on your phone. This narrows down your selection of usable clips and makes the editing process faster.

For more extensive recordings, like long interviews, you can jot down quotes and their time codes. You can also do a rough cut straight form your camera roll: trim the beginning and end of videos, flip, or rotate them. This way, you create a rough cut of usable quotes from lengthy interviews.

By selecting and rough trimming the footage beforehand, you often get a good sense of the final video, and the puzzle of putting everything together already begins!

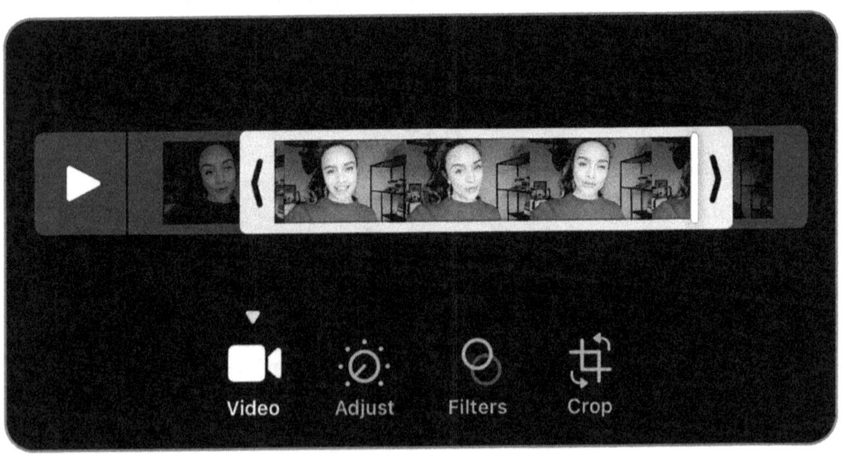

Open a video in your cameraroll and go to 'edit' to crop, cut, mirror, switch volume off, and change the colors

3. LAY THE FOUNDATION: THE PERSON OR PEOPLE.

If you have one or more people speaking on camera, that's probably going to be the foundation for your video. From the previous step, you likely have a good idea of which quotes or clips work well.

Now it's time to use these to form the foundation of your video. Open your video editing app and import the clips that form this foundation. Trim them down to the exact quotes and arrange them in the proper sequence. This step is crucial as it lays the groundwork for your video.

Enhance your foundation with visual shots. With your foundation in place—for instance, an edited interview with quotes in sequence—it's time to add extra visual shots to this base. All you need to do is choose the right B-roll shots and place them over or between the quotes. For example, if your interview discusses a fire truck, insert shots of a fire truck before or after the corresponding quote. Simple yet effective!

Adding extra shots (B-roll) to a vlog in the app InShot

4. ADD GRAPHICS AND TEXTS.

This part is often seen as the "fun" part of editing: adding transitions, texts, sounds, and more. But it's more than just embellishing your video. Adding graphics and text is the essential decoration stage of your video. Well-placed words, phrases, arrows, and banners can make your video engaging to watch. Most social media videos are watched without sound, so it's extra important to ensure viewers can follow your content. That's why strategically placed graphics and texts are crucial.

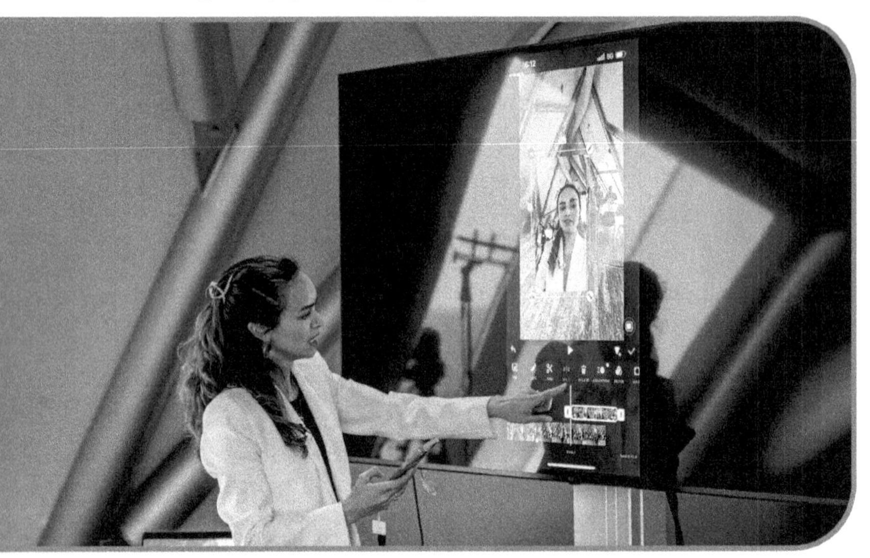

Explaining how to work with different layers in the app InShot

5. SAVE CAPTIONING AS THE FINAL STEP.

It can be a bit frustrating to have the entire video captioned, only to receive feedback that a quote needs to be removed or added. It's more efficient to complete the video, send it in for feedback, and then add captions.

Instagram expert Dot Lung using text in her video

VIDEO EDITING APPS YOU'LL WANT IN YOUR TOOLBOX

Using apps on your phone to edit videos has three big advantages:

1. **Everything happens on one device.** From shooting to editing and posting. So, there is no fuss about transferring clips to another device.

2. **Apps are far more accessible and straightforward than professional editing software.** This is great for beginners, but also for experienced editors. A more streamlined app means fewer choices to agonize over, which often leads to faster editing.

3. **Apps adapt to new trends fast.** Apps evolve fast, continually rolling out new functionalities, including advanced AI tools.

> Keep in mind, video apps are frequently updated, so my recommendations might vary over time. For a current lineup of video apps and detailed tutorial videos, you can check my Video Smart Academy, and the free masterclass at Book.VideoSmart.Academy

And remember, as you read about all the different apps in this chapter, don't feel compelled to try each one. Start with just one app. Unsure which to choose? Start with one of the most user-friendly options: InShot.

INSHOT (FREE + PAID, IPHONE/ANDROID)

This app is very easy to use and offers a ton of edit-options.

With InShot, you gain complete control over your text, including its font, color, size, duration, and even animation options. You can also add B-roll: video, photos, or a logo from your camera roll. The app lets you crop videos into different formats (vertical, square, 5:4, etc.), create top and bottom banners, and automatically generate captions in certain languages. The app works with both iOS and Android devices.

Inshot Pros:

- Free version is quite extensive and user-friendly

- Very regular updates with new tools

- Lets you work in layers: video, text, music, graphics
- Allows speed adjustment, freeze frame, and voice-over addition
- Easy removal of watermark, even in the free version
- Automatic captions available in certain languages
- Supports keyframes for professional-level editing
- Supports 4K export
- Offers a ton of fun AI video effects (mainly in the paid version)

Inshot Cons:

- Limited transition/AI effects and filters in the free version
- Music library lacks new and trending options
- It can be a bit challenging to multitask within the app
- Be prepared to watch some (long) advertisements after saving your video in the free version
- Pro tip: In the free version, you can tap the InShot logo to remove it

CAPCUT (FREE + PAID, IPHONE & ANDROID)

CapCut is a very popular video editing app and platform widely used to create social videos. CapCut is owned by ByteDance PTE. LTD, the same company behind TikTok. That's why your projects in CapCut integrate seamlessly with TikTok.

The app's features include trimming, adding text, customizing background music, splitting, adding voiceovers, and adjusting video color and brightness. CapCut's Templates section is wonderful; it offers pre-built editing templates for quick, catchy videos. These templates are wonderful to users with minimal editing experience.

There's also CapCut for Business, which has an AI-fueled script generation tool and AI-generated presenters. These virtual hosts can showcase products, offer detailed demonstrations, or narrate explainer videos for you!

<u>Capcut Pros:</u>

- Multi-layer Editing: Want to add those extra layers or B-roll shots? With CapCut, you can easily add overlays and add various transitions, effects, and automatic captions.

- Music Library: CapCut has an extensive music library with professional soundtracks and trending music. This is a huge plus point to me!

- Advanced Editing Tools: CapCut also has plenty tools for advanced video editors: non-destructive editing, masking, color correction, noise reduction, and advanced cropping features.

- CapCut for Business has an AI-powered suite—perfect to generate ads and branded content. It also supports team collaboration, so multiple members can work on a video project.

- CapCut also has an in-browser edit version and software for PC and Mac.

- Free to Use: The free version offers extensive features, while CapCut Pro gives you additional options, such as 100GB cloud storage.

Capcut Cons:

- Privacy Concerns: Many clients I work with do not want to use this app because of discussions around the app's safety and privacy measures. In 2023, for example, TikTok was fined 345 million euros ($370 million) for breaching privacy laws, regarding the processing of children's personal data in the European Union.

- Storage Drain: CapCut files can take up a lot of space on your phone. The app tends to consume storage with data from project files, cache, and exported videos.

- Ads: Advertisements may appear in the free version, which can disrupt your editing experience.

- CapCut watermark: When you export from CapCut templates to your phone (instead of posting to TikTok), the video is saved with a CapCut watermark.

- Learning Curve: CapCut might be overwhelming for beginners because of the many functions, tools, and effects. So, I'd recommend to start with basic functions like cutting and cropping before exploring advanced features of this well-packed app.

CAPTIONS

This app has evolved from a relatively simple captioning tool to a powerhouse of AI editing tools. From automatic B-roll and AI-generated music to restoring eye contact. It's no surprise that this constantly evolving app isn't free. The app is always adding new features and tools, so it's highly likely it will have new capabilities by the time you read this book.

<u>Captions Pros:</u>

- Sleek, Easy-to-Use Interface: Navigating is easy through the app's sleek design.

- Fast and Accurate Automatic Captioning: Get fast and precise automatic captioning in various templates, with the freedom to add your own fonts and colors.

- Keyframe Animations: Capture and retain viewer attention by adding dynamic keyframe animations like fast zoom in/zoom out.

- AI-Generated Video Titles: Let AI create a catchy start for your video with an automatically generated title or craft your own.

- Automatic B-roll Suggestions: This AI tool detects your speech and offers automatic suggestions for clips and pictures you can add as B-roll, an instant "say dog, see dog" effect!

- Eye Contact Correction: If you're looking off-camera (e.g., reading a script), this tool corrects eye contact to make it appear you're looking into the camera lens.

- AI Detection of Lulls or Pauses: Quickly edit and trim clips with AI's ability to detect lulls or pauses in your video.

- AI Denoising: Enhance the quality of your video clips by using AI to denoise them.

- AI Sounds and Music: Create AI sounds or custom AI music, and the app even auto-ducks music automatically for you.

- AI Voiceover: Input text and turn it into a voice-over, choose from various male or female voice-overs. Or, clone your own voice with AI!

<u>Captions Cons:</u>

- Not for Basic Edits: Captions isn't designed for foundational video edits like trimming, cropping, cutting, and adding layers, which I think are better handled by apps like InShot or CapCut. For longer edits, I'd suggest to first edit your video in another app before importing it to Captions.

- Higher Price Tag: As one of the most cutting-edge apps pioneering AI in video editing, Captions comes with a relatively higher price tag.

CANVA

You're probably familiar with Canva; maybe you use it to create brochures, banners, or presentations. Canva offers thousands of templates and makes it easy to add your own touches, like brand colors and fonts. But did you know you can also create videos in Canva using ready-made templates? And did you know Canva's Magic Studio has a bunch of user-friendly AI tools?

> When I mention InShot on stage, about 20 to 30 percent of the audience say they know the app. But when I ask about Canva, the response shoots up; 80 to 90 percent of the audience raise their hands. So, even though Canva is not a typical video editing tool, I believe it deserves a spot in this book. Canva is constantly innovating and is incredibly popular among businesses.

Canva isn't your go-to tool for heavy and creative video editing. Video editing on Canva is still in its infancy stage. But, Canva is evolving very fast, constantly adding new video and AI tools. Plus, you can seamlessly carry over your brand style to all your designs in Canva, and it's easy to collaborate on a project with multiple people.

Canva Pros:

- All-in-One Social Media Tool: Canva is a tool that's dedicated to versatile content creation, from videos to banners and slideshows.

- Ready-to-Go Video Templates: One of the main reasons I love Canva is the super-fast creation with easily customizable templates. Simply search for "YouTube intro," for example, to come across a ton of different video intro templates.

- Auto Video Edit: Let Canva create a video for you. Simply type a prompt, such as "3 tips to film videos with your smartphone," and Canva will automatically create a video for you with different shots with music, transitions, and text from selected images or videos.

- Magic Switch: One of my favorite tools. It lets you convert any type of format or repurpose it for another platform. For example, you can turn a presentation into a video or a video into a blog post article . . . with just one click!

- Text to Video: Simply type a prompt, and let Canva's AI tool generate an image or a video for you. I've used this tool many times to create video backgrounds or atmosphere shots.

  Now, fair warning, this is definitely a tool in development. Some AI-generated shots are jaw-droppingly stunning, while others are just plain weird. I've discovered that having some knowledge on video production and prompt-writing helps. It might take a few prompts get a good shot, but hey, at least there's no need to get out that camera!

- Simple Animation with Magic Animate: With this Canva tool, you can easily add movement or animation to your social posts to make them stand out.

- Cross-Platform Availability: Canva is accessible as both an app and in-browser tool. So, you can start working from the Canva app and finish the project on your computer or the other way around!

- Team Collaboration: Canva lets you share projects among team members. This is perfect for consistent on-brand video templates.

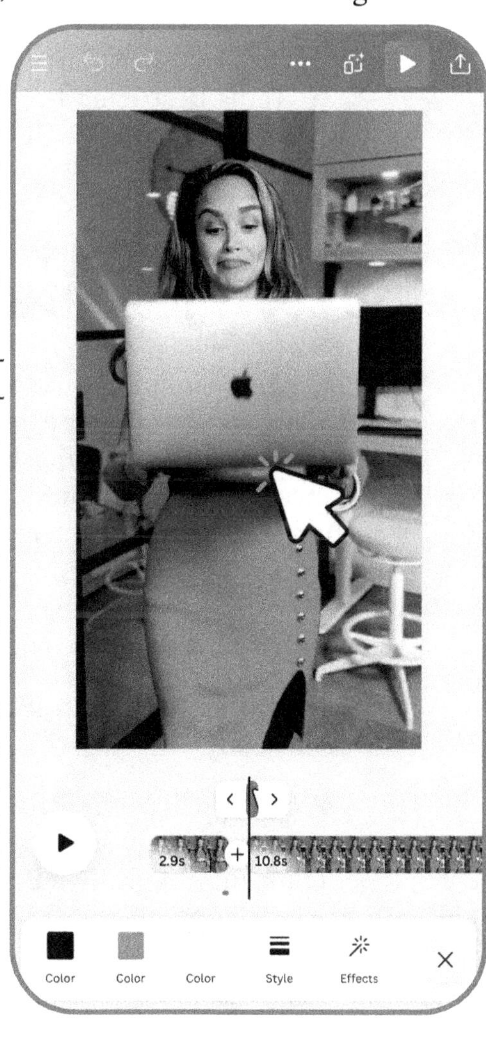

<u>Canva Cons:</u>

- Not Video-Centric: Canva is not specifically designed for video editing, although it does offer a (simple) video studio and some impressive video AI tools. I believe that Canva's video editor will develop very fast—there are probably new Canva video tools available right now as you're reading this book!

- Limited Layering Options: Canva's video editing features currently lack extensive layering options compared to most video editing apps, such as adding and editing extra videos, graphics, pictures in overlay.

- AI Tools Restricted to Pro Users: Many of Canva's AI tools within the Magic Studio are only accessible to Canva Pro users.

5 MORE (AI) TOOLS TO BOOST YOUR VIDEO EDITING

You've just been introduced to a range of different apps. So why discuss more? Because there are apps that you might not use all the time but are super handy for specific purposes. For instance, creating an impression video is much faster in Quik than in InShot. And if you're looking for an app that allows the whole communications team to easily create branded content, Vormats might be a great choice. So, here are a few additional editing apps to consider.

1. **Quik (free, Android & iPhone): to create an impression video fast**

   A nice app that does what it says it does: It makes a video quickly. Simply select a few videos and pictures, and Quik automatically edits it for you on the beat of the music! You can choose from a ton of different themes to give your video a certain look and feel, add text, and

change the order of the clips, and within a couple of minutes, you've got a fun video.

For videos with a business purpose, Quik is especially useful to create fast impression videos, event videos, or short vlogs. Calmer themes include "Raw," "Grammy," and "Lapse."

When you're editing a quote, you can adjust the length by tapping the scissors "trim," and change the audio to "boost."

The main downside of this app: It doesn't allow you to work in layers (you can't put a video over a video or a logo over your entire video, for example). It's a slideshow with a combination of pictures and videos. This app is also great for vacation, summaries of school gatherings, parties, and sports videos.

2. iMovie (free, iPhone): to create landscape videos on iPhone

A wonderful app to edit videos fast. Quickly trim, rotate, and crop your videos. iMovie is incredibly intuitive, and it also lets you edit with (limited) layers: You can place a video over a video; for example, you can put fill shots over an interview. iMovie also lets you work with green screen, add text and music to your video, change the volume of a clip, and add effects. I definitely recommend this app for beginners.

The main downside of this app, and the main reason why I hardly recommend it in video workshops anymore is because you can't export vertical video in this app. And of course, vertical video is what's used mainly on social media nowadays.

I'm writing this book in the spring of 2024, so please double check to see if the app's features have changed while you're reading this book.

3   Kinemaster (subscription, Android & iPhone): longstanding, reliable app for pros

A more traditional, extensive app that allows you to work with layers: video over video, on top of that, a logo, and on top of that, text, for example. If InShot and Capcut are a bit too "social" and "screamy" for you, then definitely check out Kinemaster. It's sleek, professional, and has a ton of professional editing options, such as animations, title screens, and fonts; you can even use keying for when you're in front of a green screen and want to change the background. It's also possible to record a voiceover within the app.

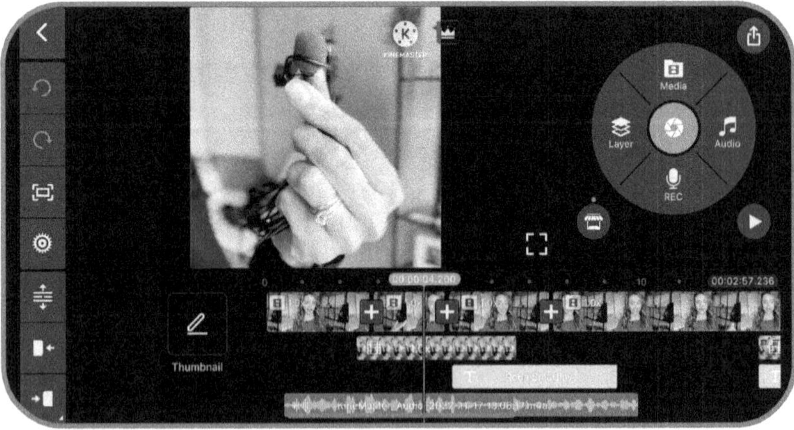

Kinemaster has a ton of audio-editing options, such as an audio envelope (which allows you to change the volume with audio points throughout the clip). The app has an extensive library with paid and free add-ons, such as different fonts, title screens, and themes. I recommend Kinemaster when you want to regularly edit company videos and need control over the look and feel. It's an intuitive app with a ton of options!

The app is free to use with the Kinemaster logo visible; to lose the logo, you have to subscribe.

4. Vormats (subscription, Android & iPhone) : designed for business videos

Vormats is an innovative video app specifically designed for business content. It's an all-in-one platform that not only helps you brainstorm your video plan or script but also guides you through the recording process. Vormats is perfect for companies that aim for consistency in how multiple people produce videos with a uniform brand style.

You can also add supporting images, company logos, and automatic subtitles. It's great for business presentations, vlogs, explainer videos, or product demonstrations.

"It's crucial that a video platform is very user-friendly for employees. This ensures that all colleagues can easily share information and knowledge in video form, regardless of their technical skills and without it taking up too much time."

—Jan-Jaap, co-founder of Vormats

5. OPUS Clip (subscription): transform long videos into short gems with one click

OPUS Clip is not an app but is definitely worth a quick mention in this book. It has saved me a ton of time. OPUS Clip is the perfect tool to generate short video clips from a longer video.

Say you have a long podcast, interview, or presentation, and you'd like to produce a bunch of short quotes or catchy bites. What used to take me hours to scour through the video and select the right bites, now OPUS Clip does it for me! Simply leave a URL to your video, and the tool will produce fifteen videos with just one click.

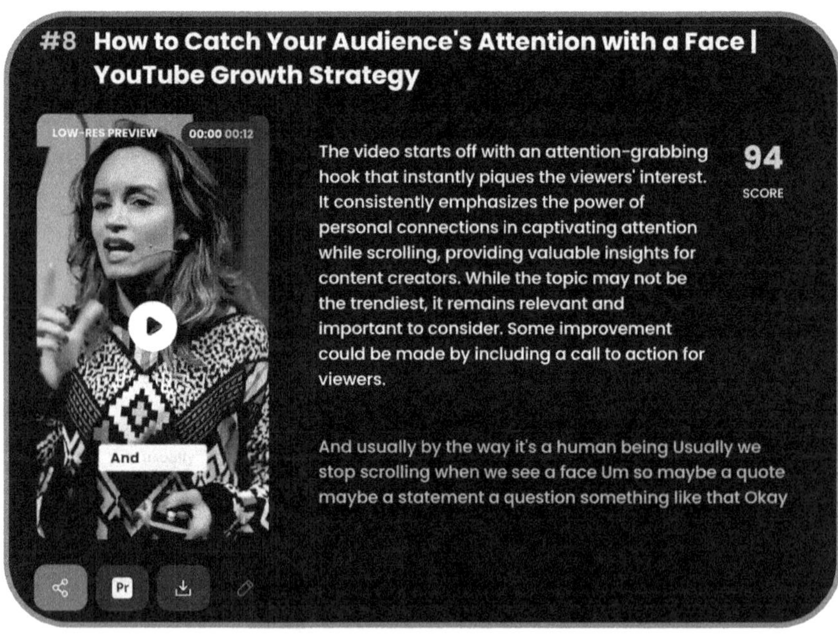

This can take your repurpose game to a whole new level. Other great features of OPUS Clip: Virality Score, which automatically generates a score to show the virality potential of each short clip; Face Tracking, where AI analyzes moving faces, ensuring you and your guest's faces will always be at the center of the video frame; Keyword Highlighter, which highlights the most valuable keywords; and AI Emoji Generator, which automatically adds relevant emojis to highlight valuable content.

NOT SURE WHAT EDITING TOOL TO USE?

Are you a bit overwhelmed with all the edit options? So many tools and apps . . . which one do you use for what type of video? I wish there was just a one-size-fits-all solution. But, since everyone works with different types of devices, and there are a ton of different audiences and different platforms, it's not easy for me to give you a simple advice without actually talking to you.

> Not every app works for every content creator.

Every time I do a masterclass or workshop, I first ask what the team is like; what is their experience, how much time do they have to create videos, and what kind of tools do they use? Also, who is your audience, and will the videos be long or short and vertical or landscape? So, based on all that information, I usually recommend an app or tool to work with.

That's why I've created this decision tree in helping you decide what app you can use for your videos.

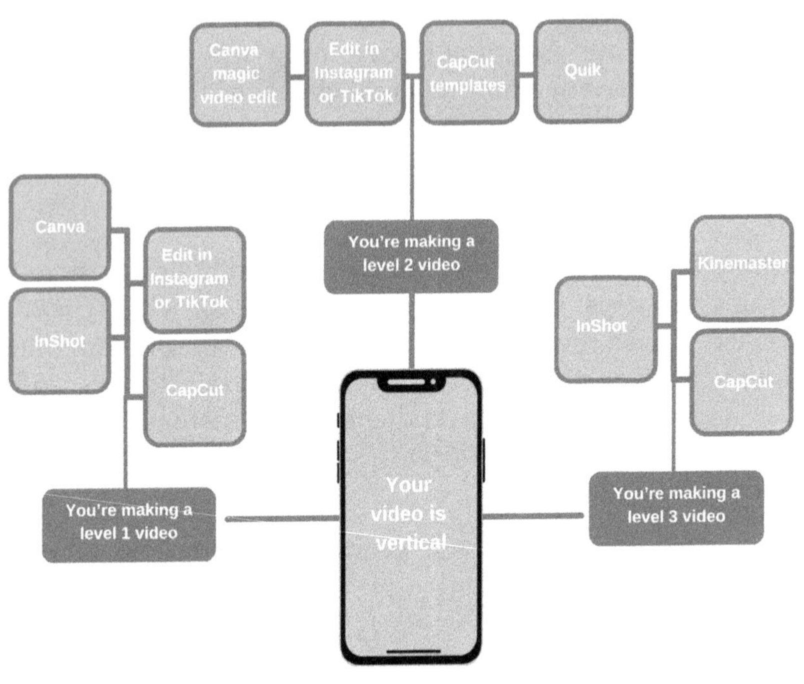

Canva magic video edit
Edit in Instagram or TikTok
CapCut templates
Quik
You're making a level 2 video
Canva
Edit in Instagram or TikTok
InShot
CapCut
You're making a level 1 video
Your video is vertical
Kinemaster
InShot
CapCut
You're making a level 3 video

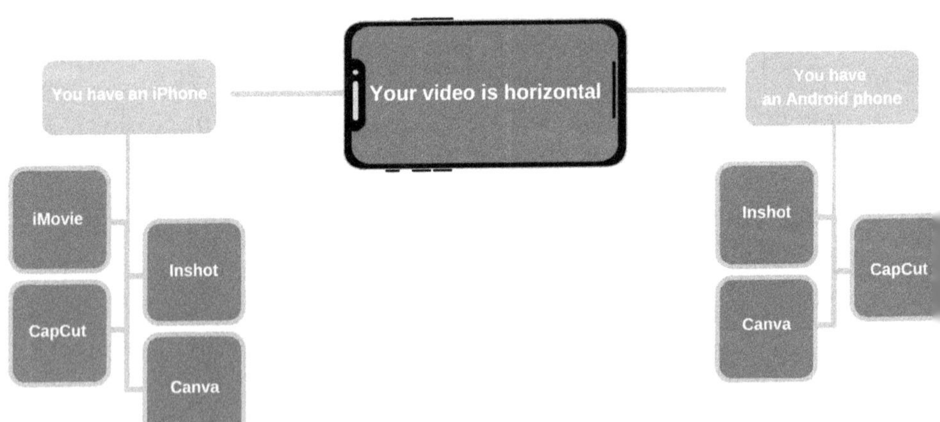

You have an iPhone
Your video is horizontal
You have an Android phone
iMovie
Inshot
CapCut
Canva
Inshot
Canva
CapCut

3 PRACTICAL EDIT - TOOLS YOU'LL WANT TO TRY

The apps introduced in this chapter use different types of AI technology to make editing faster. Now, you're about to dive deeper into some of these AI tools. Discover how you can create AI music, edit videos by typing, and produce AI voice-overs.

1. DISCOVER PERSONALIZED AI MUSIC

Ever find yourself in the endless loop of scouring for the perfect copyright-free music, only to realize it's either too long, too short, or just won't sync with your video's rhythm?

Finding the perfect music for your video can be quite the task. Enter AI music, poised to be a real game-changer. With the "AI Music" feature in the Captions app, for example, you simply specify your music preferences, and the app composes music for you, tailored to your preferences and the video you've selected.

Step one: Specify the type of music you want.

Choose your vibe: dramatic, calm, or maybe happy. It's like picking the flavor of your video—is it a corporate gig, a serious interview, or a vlog adventure?

Next, all you do is push one button, and AI automatically generates unique music for your video.

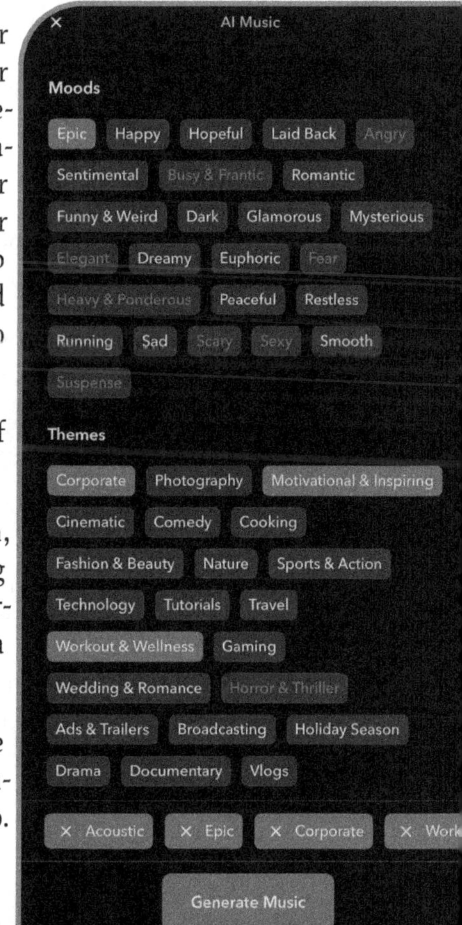

Depending on your previous preferences, the type of video, and the length of the video, AI will craft a suitable soundtrack.

It's like having your personal DJ that knows exactly what you need.

Step two: Fine-tuning.

If the AI music doesn't quite match your taste, no worries. You can adjust the knobs to match your style. You can change the intensity for different sections of music. In the app Captions, simply hit "recompose" to let the app remix the music.

Step 3: Automatic ducking.

Here's one of my favorite tools! If someone is speaking in your video, you probably want the music volume to be lower. Once they stop speaking, you probably want the music to fade back in. This can take a lot of time to do manually. Well, with AI, this is done for you. When someone talks in your video, the music's volume automatically lowers. And when no one is talking, the music will fade in automatically. Yes, the music adjusts to the speaker! Simply look for the function "automatic ducking" in apps such as Captions.

Automatic ducking in the app Captions ensures the music volume is low when someone talks in your video

Besides Captions, there are many more smartphone apps and tools, like Endlesss Studio, Amper Music, and Jukedeck that bring AI music right to your fingertips.

2. EDIT YOUR VIDEO BY SIMPLY EDITING WITH WORDS

Almost all video editing software and apps, from Adobe Premiere Pro to CapCut, work in a very similar way. You edit videos by cutting, pasting, and modifying them on a visual timeline.

But Descript is different. This tool lets you edit videos through text. Upload your video, and Descript transcribes the audio. On one side of the screen, you have your transcript, with every word spoken in the video. On the other side, your video is displayed. You then edit the video by simply adjusting the transcript. So, if you delete a sentence from the text, Descript cuts that sentence from the video. If you want to rearrange some parts, you just cut and paste the transcript, and the video follows suit.

At this moment, Descript is not available for phones (check to see if it has been updated when you're reading this book).

Although Descript is currently leading the way, other tools like Kapwing and Type Studio are also pushing the boundaries of video editing.

It's exciting to see how you can edit your videos in an entirely different manner. In a few years, you might even edit videos with voice commands. Imagine telling your phone to "delete the last sentence" or "move this segment after the intro," and it automatically happens!

3. AI POWERED VOICE-OVERS: NO MIC? NO PROBLEM!

Want to add a voice-over but don't have a mic handy? Don't feel like talking to a mic today? Or maybe you can't find the right person in your company to do a voice-over for you? Well, there's a solution now: create a voice-over for your video with AI.

The app Capcut, for example, has a variety of AI voiceovers in different languages.

Here's a super easy five-step process using CapCut:

- Open up CapCut.
- Hop over to "Text."
- Type your text.
- Select "text to speech."
- Select a voice.

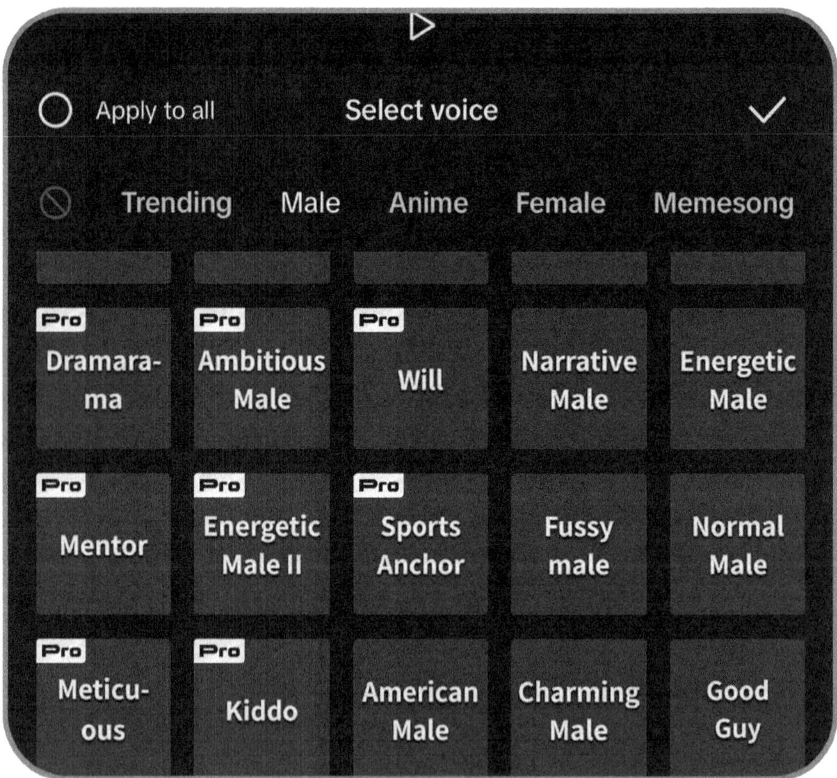

A variety of AI voices in the app Capcut

Men, women, serious vibes, or a bit goofy—they've got it all. Definitely experiment with different voices; some voices simply sound better or have a more natural pronunciation of specific words.

If you're into TikTok or Instagram Reels, you're going to love this. Some voices sound more robotic than others, so these AI voices may not be the best for professional corporate videos. But for a quick fun social clip? Absolutely perfect!

Let's take a moment to reflect. You've discovered many different editing apps and cutting-edge AI tools in this chapter. Now, let's apply what you've learned. How are you going to save time editing? Which apps or tools do you want to explore? If the options for tools and apps seem overwhelming, simply start with one app. Take a moment to jot down your thoughts and plan your next steps to incorporate these insights into your video creation process.

7
PUBLISHING &
DISTRIBUTION
IN THE AI ERA

Yes, your video is done! You've created a plan, shot the video, edited it, and now it's ready to share with your target audience. But hold on a second before you press "publish."

In this chapter, you're going to create your publishing plan. When should you post your video? What should you pay attention to when posting a video on LinkedIn, for example? And how do you optimize your video for YouTube?

If you think about the publication beforehand and plan it out, your results are going to be a whole lot different than if you just post it without any preparation.

OPTIMIZE WITH YOUR MAIN PLATFORM IN MIND

Your video is finally finished, and you can't wait to post it online. I understand you want to share it with the world immediately, but let's focus first. Let's go back to your initial goal. Before you started filming, you should have made a video plan. What was your plan? You are going to put that into practice now!

Remember the 3 Ps: People, Platform, Purpose. You start with your ideal viewer, adjust your video to the platform, and always have the final purpose in mind: What should your viewer do, think, or feel while watching your video?

> Take a moment right now to go back to your 3Ps: your people, platform, purpose. Who is your target audience? Where are you going to publish your video? And what was your original goal?

Where are you going to publish your video? Optimizing a video on YouTube is vastly different from optimizing it on Instagram. That's why we're going to look at a few guidelines for posting videos on different social media platforms.

In an ideal world, if you want to publish your video on several platforms, you would optimize your video differently for each platform. Unfortunately, most of us don't have the time and resources to create three or four different versions of one video. That's why my advice is to optimize your video with just one main platform in mind.

UPLOADING TO YOUTUBE? READ THIS FIRST!

I know many companies use YouTube to upload videos to embed them on their website or in their newsletter. But YouTube is so much more than a simple means to embed your videos elsewhere. YouTube is a social search engine. It's a place where people go to find answers, to be inspired, and to be entertained. And unlike some other platforms, YouTube is where people go to specifically watch videos.

WHEN TO POST ON YOUTUBE

It's quite simple. If you're aiming for people to discover you on YouTube through searches, you need to create videos on the topics people are searching for.

> If you want to be found on YouTube, you have to make videos people are searching for.

So, do you know what your target audience is searching for online? What are their main (recurring) questions and problems? What do people search for within your market?

> When clients want to be discovered on YouTube, the first question I ask is: "What are your viewers searching for?" For Frankwatching, I often did viewer research before creating videos on topics like "How do I delete my Facebook account?" and "How do Snapchat filters work?" For the Dutch Railways, I made instructional videos on using the public transport pass. People searched with questions such as "How do I apply for a public transport pass?" and "How does the public transport pass work?"
>
> I refer to these types of videos as "evergreen" videos; they remain relevant for a long time, which means people will keep searching on the topic. It's a solid foundation for an effective YouTube strategy.

The basic evergreen videos are made to attract new viewers, which is a good foundation for your YouTube channel. Other types of content, such as a weekly vlog, a series with case studies, or product demos, can create a bond between you and your viewers and give them a reason to come back.

WHEN NOT TO POST ON YOUTUBE

If you use your videos in B2B or education, and you mainly use videos on your website (and don't need to be found on YouTube), YouTube might not be the right platform. Or perhaps you don't want to be on YouTube because it's built on ads and lacks options on branding and customization.

Vimeo might be an interesting alternative; it's clean, less ad-focused, and has the possibility to customize the video player and put passwords on videos.

If you want to go a step further and have full control and rights over your own videos, try an enterprise video platform or video management system such as Panopto.com, VidGrid.com, or Kaltura.com. These systems give you full control over your business videos—video player look and feel, privacy, analytics, and even interaction (depending on the system, of course). These systems come with a price tag, but depending on your needs, they might be just what you're looking for.

Do you want to take a deeper dive into the YouTube algorithm? I definitely recommend following Jeremy Vest, Tim Schmoyer, and Justin Briggs.

YOUTUBE OPTIMIZATION TIPS

You can optimize a video with text, playlists, and thumbnails, but if you have bad content nobody wants to watch; it's no use. So, step one is always good content! But having said that, here are some key things to look for when you want to reach a bigger audience on YouTube.

FOCUS ON WATCH TIME

Do you know how long viewers watch your videos? That's known as watch time, a key metric YouTube considers when deciding where your video lands in its algorithm. Generally, videos with longer watch times rank higher in search results.

> It's not just about drawing viewers in with an engaging start; keeping them interested throughout is crucial.

To boost watch time, break your video into segments: "3 ways to . . .," "5 hacks for . . .," or "Top 7 . . ." Such formats are effective because even if viewers aren't captivated by step 2, they might stick around for the next one. Another popular YouTube tactic is using teasers. Place a funny moment or a powerful interview quote at the start. This can significantly increase watch time as viewers anticipate that segment.

OPTIMIZE YOUR THUMBNAILS

An intriguing thumbnail is one of the best ways to get people to watch your YouTube video. Think of your thumbnail as your business card, the main reason someone clicks on your video. And your biggest competition? Other thumbnails.

You want a thumbnail that stands out.

Avoid using YouTube's suggested screenshots; create your own with tools like Photoshop or Canva. Use a template to save time on each new thumbnail. Jeremy Vest suggests including a close-up of a face (showing emotion), high contrast colors, a few descriptive words, and subtle branding.

> Don't have a thumbnail template yet? Here's a good exercise for you. First, go to your favorite YouTube channels and observe the thumbnails. How do their thumbnails stand out? What elements do you want to incorporate in your own thumbnails? How can you integrate your branding? If you're short on time, definitely add "create thumbnail template" to your to-do list.

OPTIMIZE TEXT: TITLE, TAGS, DESCRIPTION, AND CAPTIONS

While search engines are getting smarter at understanding video content, adding text is still a great optimization strategy. It helps YouTube and Google understanding what your video is about. Essential text elements include the title, description, and tags. Craft a compelling title with keywords (40–60 characters). Write a detailed description (150–300 words) with keywords, possibly including timestamps and links.

You can use Google's Keyword Planner or Gemini for help with keywords or coming up with a catchy title, but always double-check and rewrite the text in your own style and words.

INTERACT WITH YOUR COMMUNITY

Do you want to build a community? Don't just broadcast your content; engage with your viewers. It makes sense; engaging in conversation means doing more than just transmitting.

> Interacting with your audience is not just about broadcasting your content. Engage with your viewers by asking questions, responding to comments, and sparking discussions.

Building a community can be incredibly valuable, not just for your audience and yourself but also as a signal to YouTube that your video is a hub of engagement. So, encourage your viewers to join the conversation and take the time to respond to comments.

NEXT LEVEL: PROMOTE WITH YOUTUBE LIVE

Jumping into live streaming on YouTube can change the game for your channel. It can be exciting and nerve-wracking at the same time because it's all happening live. But, because it's an unedited and real experience, it tends to pull in more engagement from your audience. Plus, YouTube gives Livestreams a nudge in its algorithm, boosting your channel's visibility.

If live streaming feels like new territory for you or if you're aiming to level up your game, Luria Petrucci from Livestreaming Pros is your go-to. I learned a ton from Luria on how to nail live video podcasting back when I was in Texas. She's got all the insights and tips to help you get the most out of live streaming.

10 THINGS TO CHECK BEFORE YOU UPLOAD TO YOUTUBE

1. Compelling Title (50–60 characters): Make sure you include relevant keywords, intrigue viewers, and keep it concise.

2. Engaging Description (150–300 words): Expand on your title, use keywords naturally, include timestamps for key points, and add a call to action (CTA).

3. Research & Include Relevant Tags (7–10): Mix popular and niche terms, avoid keyword stuffing, and stay specific to your video content.

4. Choose the Right Category & Language: Accurately categorize your video for better placement and set the correct language to reach your target audience.

5. Create a Captivating Thumbnail (1280 x 720 pixels): Use bright colors, clear text, and relevant imagery to grab attention and entice clicks.

6. Leverage Cards to Promote Other Content: Showcase related videos, playlists, or your website throughout your video to keep viewers engaged.

7. Include a Clear Call to Action (CTA): Tell viewers what you want them to do next, whether it's subscribing, liking, or visiting your website.

8. Track & Analyze Performance: Use YouTube Analytics to monitor views, engagement, demographics, and click-through rates. Identify what's working and adapt your strategy.

9. Add Closed Captions & Subtitles: Increase accessibility and reach a wider audience by including captions in multiple languages.

10. Engage with Viewers: Respond to comments, answer questions, and foster a community around your channel.

ABOUT TO POST YOUR VIDEO TO LINKEDIN? READ THIS FIRST!

LinkedIn is so much more than just a place to find work. It's a platform to connect with like-minded people, build communities, and yes, find jobs.

My first video on LinkedIn went viral. It totally caught me off guard. I didn't even catch on until a few days later when I logged back in and almost fell over. 720,000 views? How did that even happen? The next months were a whirlwind. Nearly every video I posted garnered hundreds of thousands, sometimes over a million views. My inbox was overwhelmed, and I gained nearly 25,000 followers within a year.

I discovered different methods to optimize my videos. And I also made numerous mistakes. The biggest mistake was focusing too much on numbers: more views, more followers. It initially boosted my ego, but I also learned that it diverted my attention from my business. It took some time to find the right balance.

Right now, my LinkedIn videos don't get the crazy reach like a few years ago. I'm not as active on LinkedIn as I was back then, and the algorithm also changed its preferences over videos. Sometimes, the algorithm favors videos, and other times, text posts, PDFs, or live streams.

Regardless of how the algorithm works now, I can confidently say that LinkedIn is highly effective for my business. It has given me a substantial B2B audience, helped my book Video Smart become a bestseller, and helped with visibility, trust, and credibility to get amazing international training and speaking opportunities.

Like any social network, an effective LinkedIn strategy begins with understanding your audience. Are you aiming to connect with professionals in a specific sector or market? CEOs of leading companies? Or network with individuals sharing similar professional interests? If so, LinkedIn might be a great platform for your videos.

WHEN TO POST ON LINKEDIN

When to post your video on LinkedIn? To determine the best time to post on LinkedIn, it's crucial to understand how your target audience uses the platform. LinkedIn is mainly used for professional purposes like networking, acquiring knowledge, job searching, and building brand awareness.

So, how can you create video content to be relevant to these goals? For example, can you share knowledge or professional insights? Do you want to showcase what you stand for as a potential employer? Or perhaps you aim to create personal videos for branding and networking purposes?

"One of the most common mistakes my clients make is thinking that LinkedIn videos need to be expensive and perfectly edited. However, less polished videos often perform better on LinkedIn. Successful videos are those where you genuinely get to know the speaker's personality. So, imperfections are perfectly acceptable. The message and the personal connection are what matter most."

—Wendy van Gilst, LinkedIn Strategy Consultant

How does the LinkedIn algorithm evaluate your video? The LinkedIn algorithm is constantly changing, but one constant remains: know your audience. Create content that's relevant to your audience, and engage in conversation with them. LinkedIn's basic algorithm seems to focus mainly on two key aspects:

- Relevant content

- Engagement

Relevant posts are prioritized over new posts in the regular LinkedIn feed. This means that the algorithm mainly looks at how likely it is that someone will like or share your video. It tries to predict this by looking at the user's past activities, what content they liked, shared, or commented on, and with whom they had a lot of interaction. LinkedIn now also seems to give priority to content from first-degree connections. So, you mainly see updates from people you know or follow.

> The LinkedIn algorithm used to prefer "viral" content, regardless of its relevance to the viewer. But now, the focus seems to be more on showing expert knowledge and advice that matches the viewers' interests and industries.

When posting a video on LinkedIn, it's also important to plan the timing of video posts. When is your target audience typically on LinkedIn? If you're not sure, you can experiment with different days and times. The perfect day and time to post for you depends on when your viewers are online.

THINGS TO CHECK BEFORE YOU POST ON LINKEDIN:

1. Craft a Clear Description & Title: Write a compelling description accompanying your video, starting with an attention-grabbing headline, question, or statement. Use concise bullet points to highlight key information. Incorporate relevant keywords to improve searchability and discoverability.

2. Design for Sound-Off Viewing: Many social media users watch videos without sound, so make sure captioning is on. LinkedIn supports automatic captioning when uploading.

3. Tag Relevant Businesses and People: Tag individuals or companies mentioned in your video to enhance visibility and encourage interactions. But, ensure tags are relevant to avoid being perceived as spam.

4. Optimize Timing for Maximum Reach: Post your video at times when your audience is most active online to maximize engagement and increase visibility in the LinkedIn algorithm.

5. Use Relevant Hashtags: Include relevant hashtags in your video description to categorize your content and make it easier for users to discover.

6. Engage with Comments and Interactions: Monitor and respond to comments and interactions on your video promptly to foster engagement and build relationships with your audience.

7. Optimize Thumbnail Image: Choose an eye-catching thumbnail image for your video that accurately represents the content and entices users to click. A visually appealing thumbnail can significantly increase click-through rates and engagement.

8. Encourage Engagement and Shares: In your video, include a clear call-to-action encouraging viewers to like, comment, and share the content. Higher levels of engagement signal to the LinkedIn algorithm that the video is valuable and relevant, leading to increased visibility and reach.

9. Did your video flop? Take it down and try again later. This might be somewhat controversial advice, but it often works well for me. If I don't get some traction on the video within an hour, I delete it and repost the same video at a later time. More often than not, the video then performs a lot better!

10. Analyze Performance and Iterate: Regularly review analytics to assess the performance of your videos. Use insights to refine your strategy, experiment with different approaches, and continuously improve your content for better SEO results on LinkedIn.

I have published a video on LinkedIn every day for two consecutive years. It has given me a dedicated platform and community. It has also opened doors, including a request to write for Forbes, speaking engagements around the world, and representing cool brands like WeWork and Adobe.

—Goldie Chan, top LinkedIn Content Creator

ABOUT TO POST YOUR VIDEO ON INSTAGRAM? READ THIS FIRST!

So much has changed over the past years on Instagram. First, photos were all the rage. Then there was a huge push for video. Now, we've seemed to reach a phase where things are going to balance out a bit and not a single-content approach. While Reels still get high reach, Instagram's recent changes prefer engagement over pure video push. As content creator or entrepreneur, this means you need to diversify your content.

> A good Instagram strategy doesn't mean just posting reels. It means engaging with your community through a mix of media: high-quality photos, engaging Reels, interactive Stories, and strategic Live videos.

Focus on sparking conversations, responding to comments, and optimizing each format for its strengths. Experiment, track results, and prioritize authentic connections to thrive on the evolving Instagram landscape.

DITCH THE BUSINESS APPROACH ON INSTAGRAM

Unlocking Instagram's algorithm can be one of the most challenging tasks for businesses. My main advice is to ditch the business approach to Instagram. Yes, I know I may be losing a few of you with these words, but stick with me. Think of it like being a party host who wants everyone to have a good time.

Instagram favors engaging content that sparks conversations, not just passive watching. So, stop the sales pitches and make it more fun and personal: opt for informative Reels, interactive Stories, and exciting Live Streams. Optimize each format for its strengths, use trending sounds and hashtags, and remember to respond to comments and build your community. In short: embrace the shift from pure sales push to meaningful connections.

INSTAGRAM ALGORITHM

The Instagram algorithm is constantly changing, but there are a few things that seem to stay the same. Videos that receive a lot of interaction and watch time appear to be preferred by the algorithm. It's not just about the numbers but about real connections. So, optimize your video strategy for engagement. These five crucial aspects will transform your videos, so they ignite conversations and help you build a loyal community:

1. Engagement over Everything: Forget chasing endless views. The current algorithm prioritizes videos that spark active engagement. Focus on content that prompts comments, replies, shares, and saves. Ask questions, use interactive elements, and actively reply to viewers.

2. Diversify Your Format Frenzy: While Reels remain powerful, don't neglect other formats. Use high-quality photos with engaging captions, post Stories for real-time updates and polls, and consider doing Live sessions for in-depth interactions.

3. Content with Context Is King: Don't just post random videos. Align your content with your brand message, target audience, and platform-specific trends. Offer valuable information, showcase your personality, or entertain while subtly promoting your offerings.

4. Be a Master of Each Format: Understand the strengths and weaknesses of each video format. Keep Reels short and impactful, prioritize clear visuals and editing in Stories, and offer exclusive behind-the-scenes insights or product demos in Live sessions.

5. Analyze, Adapt, and Amplify: Don't set it and forget it. Track your video performance, analyze engagement metrics, and adapt your strategy based on what resonates with your audience. A/B test different approaches, hashtags, and posting times to continuously improve.

The key thing to remember is that Instagram videos are about connecting with your audience, not just racking up views. My advice is to prioritize engagement and diversifying your format mix.

When you create relevant content to your audience and continuously analyze results, you can optimize your videos for success and build a thriving community on Instagram. And, don't forget that you can start small: simply start with level one and level-two videos, photos, and stories. Don't make it too complicated for yourself!

"One big learning I've had in my journey is to always do your own thing, in your own style, and make your own lane. This also applies to your Instagram content. Your uniqueness is how you attract the right community."

—Dot Lung, Instagram & Personal Brand Strategist

10 THINGS TO CHECK WHEN POSTING YOUR VIDEO ON INSTAGRAM

1. Prioritize Interaction: Ask questions, start with a statement, and highlight comments from your community. Foster relationships and engagement by responding to likes, comments, and direct messages.

2. Use Captions and Subtitles: Incorporate captions or subtitles in your videos to cater to users who watch with the sound off. This ensures accessibility and enhances engagement.

3. Post at the Right Time: Share your videos when your target audience is most active on the platform. Experiment with different days and times to find the optimal posting schedule for your specific audience.

4. Use Hashtags and Locations: Include relevant hashtags and locations to enhance discoverability. Aim for about nine hashtags per post, as recommended by SproutSocial.

5. Tag People and Companies: Tag individuals and businesses relevant to your content to increase visibility and potential engagement. However, be mindful of over-tagging to avoid being perceived as spam.

6. Use Trending Audio/Filters: For a level one or level-two video, try to use trending audio, if possible. Before you upload, discover which tunes are currently trending (preferably under 10,000 uses), and add one of those to your video.

7. Post Video in Instagram Stories: After you've posted your video, add it to your stories to reach the people who mainly check stories. Incorporate locations, hashtags, and interactive features to encourage interaction and increase visibility.

8. Be human for ten minutes: Right after posting a new video, take ten minutes to engage with responses on older posts and content from other creators. It's all about creating true connections, not just broadcasting!

9. Livestreaming: Consider hosting livestream events to connect with your audience in real-time. Ensure you have a compelling reason to go live and adequately prepare for the broadcast.

10. Monitor Analytics and Adjust Strategy: Regularly review insights and analytics to track performance and identify areas for improvement. Use data to refine your strategy and optimize future video content.

> Do you want to get more insight into your Instagram account? A quick check at igaudit.io can tell you the basics of how you're doing: average number of likes, interaction, number of fake followers, and language of your followers.

ABOUT TO POST YOUR VIDEO TO TIKTOK? READ THIS FIRST!

Let's talk TikTok, the king of lightning-fast entertainment. Forget polished perfection, TikTok thrives on raw energy and bite-sized brilliance. Here's your quick guide to unlocking this dynamic platform and captivating Gen Z (and beyond) with your brand.

DITCH THE SALES PITCH

Leave your sales pitch at the door; it won't work on TikTok. This platform isn't about pushing products; it's about new trends, cool challenges, creative videos, and raw emotion. Attention spans are short, so make sure your videos grab attention from the start and keep them brief. Hook scrolling viewers with captivating visuals, catchy music, and clear narratives.

> TikTok is famous for its funny dances and fun challenges, but you don't have to dance to get noticed on TikTok.

Find what works for you, your brand, and most importantly, your audience. And if it fits, you can jump on trending songs, popular hashtags, and new challenges.

When the Dutch Eurovision song "Europapa" suddenly became a huge hit, many businesses cleverly tapped into this trend on TikTok. Companies filmed dancing colleagues along the theme of "since Europapa dropped." A paint shop highlighted the blue paint in Europapa, and various companies jumped on the "12 points from us" trend—like the Dutch store Kwantum showcasing twelve different cushions. So, you can put your own spin on an existing challenge or trending audio to be visible to a younger audience.

So, for TikTok, don't create traditional videos with logos, brand styles, and intros. Instead, opt for subtle branding and focus primarily on content that resonates with younger viewers. Don't be afraid to show off the personality and values of your brand. Be genuine, use humor, respond to comments, answer questions, and engage in conversations.

TikTok isn't about pushing products. It's about sparking trends, joining challenges, and entertaining audiences with creative storytelling.

"Look straight into the camera lens and share your best tips. On TikTok, you talk to your audience as if you're speaking to your best friend—keep it real, no commercial vibes."

Kirsten Jassies, Short Video
Expert & Author of 'Tiktologie

10 THINGS TO CHECK WHEN POSTING TO TIKTOK

1. Community over Conversion: Focus on conversations and building relationships with your audience rather than simply trying to get conversions.

2. Optimize Video with Text Placement: Grab viewers' attention by strategically placing your main text to catch the viewer's eye. My advice is to put the main text in the upper part of your video, and make sure the captions are not too far down the screen for maximum visibility and readability.

3. Edit Text in Capcut or TikTok: If possible, optimize the text in your video by adding the text to your video in Capcut or TikTok. TikTok can read the text that you've added, which canhelp with compatibility and visibility.

4. Jump on Trending Audio, Hashtags, and Challenges: Stay updated on trending audio tracks, hashtags, and challenges within your niche or industry. Use these trends into your content to increase discoverability and engagement.

5. Use Hashtags and Locations: Include relevant hashtags and locations in your video captions. Research and use a mix of popular (general) and niche (industry-specific) hashtags. My advice is to aim for three to seven relevant hashtags.

6. Compelling Caption: Craft a caption (under 150 characters), using relevant keywords and a strong call to action (CTA). Include questions, storytelling elements or humor to grab attention.

7. Add a thumbnail: Design an eye-catching thumbnail that reflects your video's content and invites viewers to click. My advice is to use clear visuals, close-up shots, and bright colors.

8. Use Duets and Stitches for Collaboration: Work together with other creators by using the duet and stitch features. This can help in expanding your reach.

9. Be human for ten minutes: Right after you post a new video, take ten to fifteen minutes to engage with your audience by responding to comments, likes, and shares promptly. Encourage conversations to strengthen your community.

10. Incorporate Analytics into Your Strategy: Use TikTok's analytics tools to track the performance of your videos. Take some time to check out metrics such as views, likes, shares, and comments regularly, to gain insights into what truly resonates with your audience. Then, adapt your strategy based on these insights to optimize future videos.

Building a successful TikTok presence takes time and effort. Be patient, experiment, and have fun! The more you engage with the platform and its community, the more your videos, and your brand, will thrive.

ARE YOU ABOUT TO POST A VIDEO TO FACEBOOK? READ THIS FIRST!

Facebook is a massive platform where people hang out, communities chat, games get played, and businesses use videos to get noticed and talked about.

When it comes to deciding when to post on Facebook, the big question is: Are your people actually active on Facebook? I mean, sure, they might have accounts, but do they actually use them?

If your target audience is indeed spending time on Facebook, then it's all about figuring out how to grab their attention with videos.

IT'S ALL ABOUT VALUABLE CONNECTIONS AND INTERACTION

Optimization for your videos on Facebook starts with good content. There's no point in optimizing keywords, tags, and descriptions if the video itself isn't worth watching.

> The algorithm for video discoverability on Facebook has changed significantly over the years. Nowadays, simply pushing your videos won't work. Facebook focuses on valuable connections and interactions.

So, how can you make sure your video is picked up by the Facebook algorithm?

- Previously, the algorithm preferred videos with lots of views, regardless of interaction or engagement. Now, it's more important if viewers also react, share, and save your video. So, make sure your video invites to interact.

- Facebook prioritizes first-degree connections. Videos from people you directly know or follow now appear more prominently in your feed than updates from other (second or third-degree) connections.

- Videos shared by groups and pages have less organic reach unless they generate high engagement.

Facebook also actively promotes live videos, giving them increased visibility in feeds and search results. Not surprisingly, following along the TikTok trend, shorter videos are preferred also on Facebook. While Facebook supports longer formats, videos under three minutes tend to perform better.

10 THINGS TO CHECK BEFORE
POSTING YOUR VIDEO TO FACEBOOK

1. Focus on Conversation: On Facebook, your video thrives on interaction. So, focus on conversations and building relationships with your viewers.

2. Caption craft: Write engaging captions (under 150 characters). Want to boost interaction? Start off with a question or statement.

3. Captivating Thumbnail: Create an attention-grabbing thumbnail that accurately represents your video's content and invites viewers to watch your video. My advice is to use an action-shot or closeup, and preferably vivid colors to stand out in the Facebook newsfeed.

4. Post at the right time: Not sure when your audience is online? Experiment with different days and times to find when your target audience is most active.

5. Use Relevant Hashtags: Include relevant hashtags to increase discoverability of your video. Research popular and niche hashtags (perhaps with Google's Gemini) related to your content and incorporate them in the text of your post.

6. Tag Relevant Pages and People: Tag relevant pages, individuals, or businesses mentioned in your video to increase visibility and engagement on Facebook.

7. Be Human for Ten Minutes: Right after you post a new video, take ten to fifteen minutes to engage with your audience by responding to comments, likes, and shares. Dive into the conversation, ask for questions and opinions, and simply engage with your viewers.

8. Post Video in Stories: After you've posted your video, add it to your Facebook stories to reach the people

who mainly check stories. Don't forget to add locations, hashtags, and interactive features such as polls.

9. Go Live and Run Contests/Giveaways: Ready for the next step? Consider hosting live sessions for product launches, demos, or Q&A to get some real-time connection with your viewers.

10. Monitor Performance: Track the performance of your video using Facebook Insights or other analytics tools. Monitor metrics such as view time, engagement, and shares to gauge the effectiveness of your content. Use insights to refine your strategy and optimize future videos for better results.

HOW AI HELPS WITH OPTIMIZING AND PUBLISHING YOUR VIDEO CONTENT

Your video is done and ready to be uploaded online. But how do you craft a catchy caption that accurately represents your video content and sparks attention? Do you find it challenging to write an engaging caption for your video? This is where AI tools can guide you in the right direction.

I was blown away. I hit one button, and the perfect title and summary for my video popped on my screen. It was early 2023, and I hadn't started using AI for my captions. I was editing a video in the Captions app when all of a sudden, AI-generated text, along with relevant hashtags, appeared out of nowhere. Amazing!

TITLE

Translate Posts in Canva with AI

DESCRIPTION

Did you know you can easily translate your Canva posts? Here's a Dutch post I made for my book, but with just a few clicks, I can now translate it to English! 🌍🌎🌏

HASHTAGS

#canvatranslation #multilingualposts #languageoptions #easytranslations #visualmarketing #socialmediatips #marketinghacks

Edit

Duplicate

Download

*Social media caption automatically
created by AI in the app Captions*

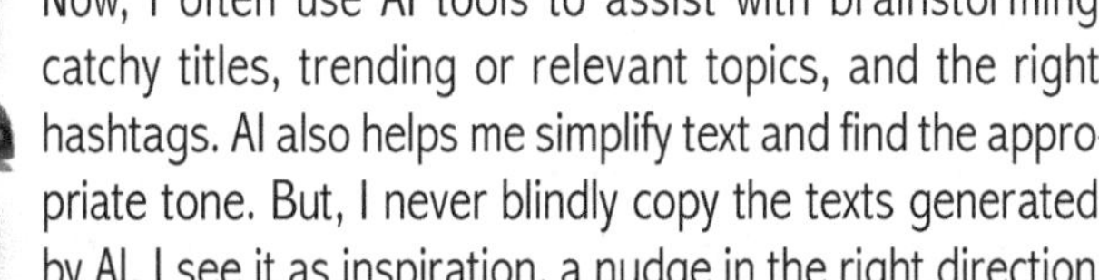

Now, I often use AI tools to assist with brainstorming catchy titles, trending or relevant topics, and the right hashtags. AI also helps me simplify text and find the appropriate tone. But, I never blindly copy the texts generated by AI. I see it as inspiration, a nudge in the right direction.

HOW GEMINI CAN HELP YOU IN CRAFTING A VIDEO CAPTION

Describe your video's content, and Gemini can suggest ideas for the caption—the text that accompanies your video on socials. Gemini can even propose relevant keywords and trending hashtags. Here are three practical ways Gemini can assist you:

1. **Capturing Attention:**

    - Gemini can assist you in crafting compelling headlines that grab attention and pique viewers' curiosity.

    - Interested in starting with a question or statement? Ask Gemini for some examples, perhaps including questions related to popular search queries.

2. **Providing Clarity:**

    - Struggling to keep your text short? Put your (longer) text into Gemini, specify your goal, your company and target audience, and request a shorter version.

    - Gemini can help convert your text into a casual or formal language that resonates with your target group.

3. **Optimization:**

    - Ask Gemini for relevant hashtags for your video and target audience.

    - Want to tap into current events or trends? Tell Gemini about your video's content and your target audience, and ask for news, trends, or current themes you could leverage.

    - Gemini can also give you ideas on the length of your caption, which keywords it should include, and which accounts you might tag for increased visibility.

> Gemini is an incredible brainstorming partner, but not a replacement for your own writing. So, never just copy-paste what Gemini offers you. Always do a fact-check. Consider your chat with Gemini as inspiration, a springboard to an idea that you'll then spin with your own unique twist.

CAPTIONS APP READS YOUR VIDEO TO CREATE CAPTIONS, TEXT, AND TITLES

Imagine this: you upload your video, and within a few seconds, AI generates an engaging caption for you, complete with a catchy title, keywords, and hashtags.

Tools like the Captions app use AI technology to help you with your text and captions:

- First, the app uses advanced speech recognition algorithms to transcribe the audio content of your video. It listens to the words spoken in your video.

- The transcribed text is then fed into NLP models. These models analyze the language to understand the context, sentiment, and key points being conveyed.

- Using insights from NLP, the AI engine generates a summary of your video's content in the form of a title and keywords.

- Finally, the AI combines all this information to create a catchy and engaging caption for your viewers, taking into account the tone of the video, the target audience, and any trending topics to generate content that resonates with your viewers.

The Captions app is definitely one to watch. I've been using this app for years and have seen it evolve from a simple captioning tool into an AI powerhouse with smart tools for editing your videos.

HOW AI CAN HELP PREDICT THE SUCCESS OF YOUR SOCIAL VIDEO

What if you could predict whether a video would hit the mark or not? There are AI tools who predict how successful your video will be on social media, such as Opus Clips.

Opus Clips is mainly known for its ability to automatically trim long videos. Say you've filmed an in-depth interview, a lengthy presentation, or a workshop that lasts an hour. How do you turn this long video into engaging short videos?

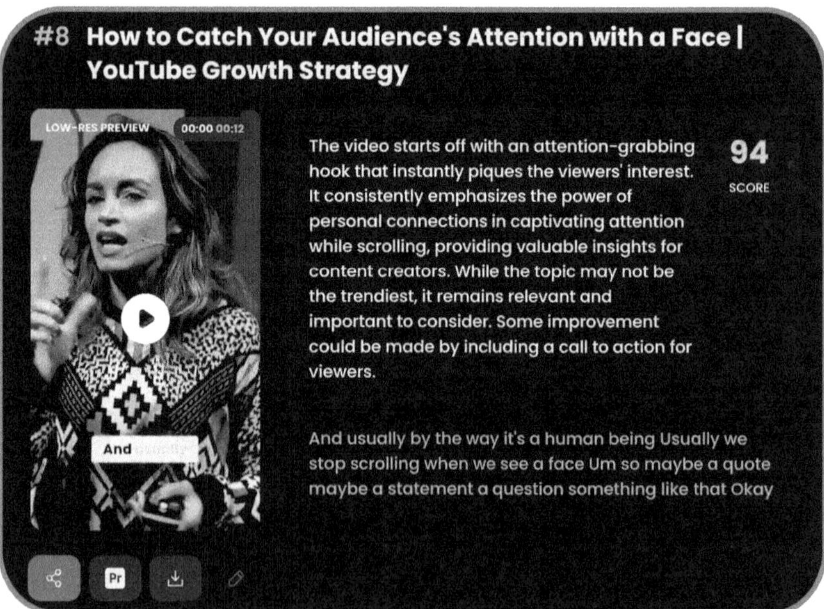

Opus Clips analyzes your video and predicts how successful it will be

Opus Clips can quickly generate ten to fifteen short clips from your long video. This innovative tool not only creates custom short clips for various platforms (like Instagram Reels, TikTok, YouTube Shorts) but also analyzes your content and predicts its potential performance.

Here's how Opus Clips works:

- Upload your long video. Give Opus Clips ten to fifteen minutes, and you'll receive an email notification that your short clips have been generated. The tool automatically optimizes the clips for popular social media platforms.

- Not all platforms are created equal. Opus Clips adjusts the length, canvas size, and style of each clip based on the platform you select, maximizing engagement on Instagram, TikTok, or YouTube.

- Opus Clips doesn't just cut videos; it analyzes content using AI algorithms. Based on factors like humor, storytelling, trends, and audience, it generates a "Social Buzz Score," predicting how well each clip would perform on social media.

> Use AI tools as a source of inspiration. Don't just copy and paste the output. See it as a good starting point from which you add your own facts, stories, and sentiment!

DON'T FORGET THIS FINAL STEP: CHECK IN WITH YOUR VIEWERS

Whew, you've done all the steps! From video planning to filming, editing, optimizing, and publishing your videos, now you're done, right? Well, not quite. There's one very important last step you should never miss.

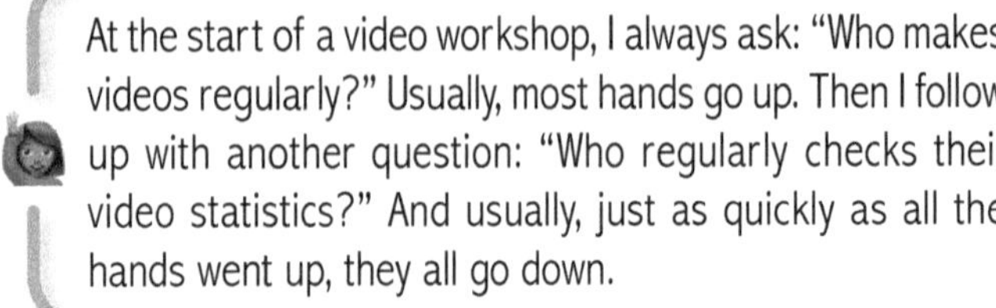

If you have a goal, doesn't it make sense to check whether you're on track to reach that goal? For example, if you want to get fit, you can make a plan to start running every other day. You probably also want to know whether it's working by checking if your time or duration improves.

Key moments for audience retention

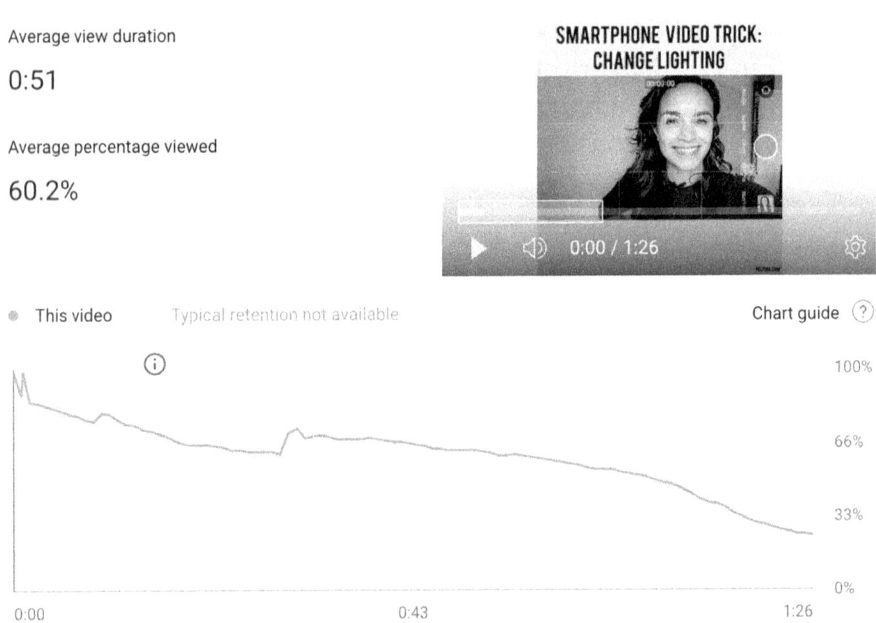

Audience retention in YouTube can show you how long your viewers keep watching your videos

The same principle applies to your video strategy. After creating a video vision and plan, it's crucial to schedule regular moments to dive into your video statistics. This could be once every fourteen days, for example.

And by checking statistics, I don't just mean looking at the amount of views. If you truly want to get to know your audience, you have to delve deeper:

- Who's watching your videos? Are your viewers the target audience you had in mind when you crafted your video plan?
- How long do people stick around to watch your videos? Does this align with your original plan?
- At what point do viewers drop off, and what's happening in the video at that moment?
- Are they watching on laptops or mobile devices?
- Which videos receive a lot of interaction, and which are saved or forwarded?
- How do viewers find your videos (through a search, another video, a website, etc.)?

These insights reveal a lot about your viewers' behavior and whether your original plan is effective. Some platforms, like YouTube, offer incredibly detailed analytics, while others, like LinkedIn, provide a more basic overview. Yet, even fundamental statistics can help you understand your audience and evaluate the success of your video strategy.

> Get to know your viewer behavior. No one else but your viewers can tell you if your videos resonate well.

If you've posted a video across multiple channels or platforms, analytics can also help you determine where the video performed best and where it didn't. Keep in mind that each network measures differently. For example, an organic view on Facebook is counted after three seconds; on Instagram Stories, it's counted as soon as it's opened; and on YouTube, it's usually around thirty seconds (this is a bit more complex but gives you an idea that statistics are measured differently).

HOW DO YOU MAKE SURE TO REGULARLY CHECK IN ON YOUR VIEWERS' BEHAVIOR?

Simply set a regular time to analyze your video statistics. This way, you'll know whether your current video approach is effective or if adjustments are needed. The goal you initially set was your guide in creating your videos, so it makes sense to periodically check if you're on the right track.

> Final exercise! Take out your calendar and schedule a regular time to analyze your video statistics. Typically, an hour once a month is sufficient, depending on your goals, of course. See it as a moment to check in with your viewers. You've set a goal, developed a plan, filmed, edited, and posted the videos online. Now, it's time to check in with your viewers. What can your viewers tell you?

CONCLUSION
WHAT IS TO COME

People often ask if I'm afraid to lose my job. AI machines will soon produce complete business videos, so won't my work become obsolete?

There's quite a bit of fear around. Whenever something unknown and new emerges, and its implications aren't yet clear, it's indeed daunting. I also find it overwhelming to keep up with all the new technologies and stay informed about all the new tools. It's almost impossible, even for me, though I work with new tools daily.

The most important lesson I've learned so far from experimenting with the latest apps, AI technology, and observing content creators who rely too heavily on AI is: don't make it about the technology.

> Technology shouldn't be the foundation of your content. Your story, your knowledge, your character, that's what it's all about. The ability to genuinely connect with your viewer, empathize with your audience, and creatively think outside the box, that's the foundation for good content. And I think it will remain that way for a long time.

So, by all means, use those handy smartphone apps, jump on fun new challenges, and utilize smart tools to make videos faster. These tools can save you an incredible amount of time. And there will probably be even more tools that will make your work even quicker and easier. But remember that these tools are just a way to achieve your goal. They don't form the foundation. Don't let the tools make the content for you; you are the creator, the creative mind; you bring the human touch.

> The art is to move along with technology, understand which tools you can employ to make your work smarter and quicker, and recognize the dangers and consequences of using certain technologies.

It's incredibly important to continue learning how these new technologies work and how you can responsibly use them for your business or brand. So, always stay true to your base: your viewer, the platform, and your goal. Who do you want to reach? What's happening in your viewer's world, and how can you create videos around that?

Move with the times and keep your knowledge up to date. If you make videos this way, you really don't need to be afraid of all the changes. On the contrary.

I think it's a great time to be a content creator. There's so much innovation, movement, and an incredible number of tools and ways being devised to make content creation smarter and quicker.

And if you can create content faster, you have time left for the truly important things in life. For me, that's my husband Rik and our three wonderful children: Liam, Davin, and Noa.

Pelpina

A big thank you to the bright minds I was able
to interview and quote in this book.

ABOUT THE AUTHOR

Pelpina helps companies generate visibility, sales, and authority by creating videos with impact. She has trained thousands of professionals worldwide to create videos using smartphones, and is the founder of the Video Smart Academy.

Her first book, *Video Smart – Make Smartphone Videos like a Pro*, made the Amazon bestseller's list.

Pelpina offers a unique combination of expertise with years of experience in journalism, TV, and online video, combined with practical knowledge on apps, social media, and content marketing.

On any regular day, you can find Pelpina hosting a video, filming, editing, making video strategy plans, and sharing her knowledge through speaking and (online) coaching. Pelpina and her husband Rik lived in Texas for ten years, and now live in the Netherlands with their three children, Liam, Davin and Noa.

Find more on Pelpina at Pelpina.com.

FREE TRAINING

Grab your phone and notebook, Pelpina will let you experience how to make your own business videos in this 45-minute hands-on training.

- Inspiring video examples
- Ideas to simplify your business videos
- Practical filming exercises
- Discover how to make your videos less complex
- Learn how to use AI to come up with video ideas
- Learn to edit your smartphone videos faster

Book.VideoSmart.Academy